# TEACHING MUSIC

# *THE HUMAN EXPERIENCE*

BY

SHIRLEY MULLINS

**Sole Selling Agent:**
The Boston Music Company
172 Tremont Street
Boston, Massachusetts 02111

**Printed by:**
Tarrant Dallas Printing
Dallas, Texas

Copyright 1985, 1998 by Shirley Strohm Mullins. All rights reserved
Published 1985. Second Edition 1998
Printed in the United States of America

2001 2003 2006    10 9 8 7 6 5 4

Requests for permission to make copies of any part of the book should be mailed to: Shirley Mullins, 537 Ridgecrest Drive, Yellow Springs, Ohio 45387. No part of this book may be reproduced in any form without permission from the author.

Grateful acknowledgment is made to The Instrumentalist Company, Northfield, Illinois, for permission to reprint the following articles: "Students Teaching Students," copyright 1980 by The Instrumentalist Company, reprinted by permission from *The Instrumentalist* (October, 1980); and "Motivation," copyright 1981 by The Instrumentalist Company, reprinted by permission from *The Instrumentalist* (November, 1981). Grateful acknowledgment is also made to City Lights Books, San Francisco, California, for permission to use the quote from the book, *Isadora Speaks*, copyright 1981 by City Lights Books.

Photographers: Charlie Ayres, page 21; The Concord String Quartet by Wayne Brill (Interlochen Center for the Arts), page 22; Tebby Stanley, page 36; Bill Garlow, page 43; Wayne Brill (Interlochen Center for the Arts), page 51; Courtesy of the *Xenia Daily Gazette*, page 61; Bruce Goldflies, page 62; Arthur Mullins, page 69; John Froschauer, courtesy of the *Springfield Newspaper*, page 74; Bill Mullins, page 79; Stanley Bernstein, page 88; courtesy of the *Yellow Springs News*, page 92.

Cover: David Battle Designs, Inc.

Back cover photo: Dennie Eagleson

ISBN 0-9616262-0-8

*"Once you are interested in shaping children's lives, you will never be interested in anything else again. There is nothing greater."*

*Isadora Duncan*
*Isadora Speaks*

# CONTENTS

Preface . . . . . . . . . . . . . . . . . . . . . . . . . . . . . . vii
Acknowledgments . . . . . . . . . . . . . . . . . . . . . . ix
I. Coping With Conflict . . . . . . . . . . . . . . . . . . . . 1
II. Transfusions . . . . . . . . . . . . . . . . . . . . . . . . . 5
III. Administrators . . . . . . . . . . . . . . . . . . . . . . . 10
IV. Discipline . . . . . . . . . . . . . . . . . . . . . . . . . . 15
V. Stage Presence . . . . . . . . . . . . . . . . . . . . . . 19
VI. Counselor and Friend . . . . . . . . . . . . . . . . . . 24
VII. Flexibility . . . . . . . . . . . . . . . . . . . . . . . . . . 27
VIII. Attitude . . . . . . . . . . . . . . . . . . . . . . . . . . . 31
IX. Motivation . . . . . . . . . . . . . . . . . . . . . . . . . 42
X. Contests . . . . . . . . . . . . . . . . . . . . . . . . . . 53
XI. Teaching Gifted Students . . . . . . . . . . . . . . . 59
XII. Recruiting . . . . . . . . . . . . . . . . . . . . . . . . . 72
XIII. Funding . . . . . . . . . . . . . . . . . . . . . . . . . . 80
XIV. Working With the Press . . . . . . . . . . . . . . . . 86
XV. A Shoestring Artist Series . . . . . . . . . . . . . . . 90
XVI. Utopia? Not Quite! . . . . . . . . . . . . . . . . . . . 95
Epilogue . . . . . . . . . . . . . . . . . . . . . . . . . . . 101
Conclusion . . . . . . . . . . . . . . . . . . . . . . . . 111
Index . . . . . . . . . . . . . . . . . . . . . . . . . . . . 113

# PREFACE

There are no adequate means of preparing teachers for the barrage of stress, conflict and problems awaiting them in the classroom. National education's attention to such concerns as burnout, assault and drugs tells the sad tale: it's not easy being a teacher in today's schools.

Yet, there is a desperate need for dedicated, loving teachers. It is for you that I have written this book.

. . . For you, the young, inexperienced teacher—a little scared, wondering how things will go—so you will know that we all have doubts.

. . . For you, the veteran teacher, so you might smile or nod feeling something with my plight on that particular day, remembering your own "variation on a theme."

. . . For you, the parents of that new teacher. How I share what you've experienced to reach this day—the worry, the patience, the love and pride.

. . . For you, the professor, preparing student teachers for successful careers, knowing full well the problems just ahead.

. . . For you, the students, who shared these moments with me, remembering what we felt together.

There's a small, handwritten sign on my desk which says "Write the Truth." I have tried my best to do just that. The incidents in this book really happened, and here we are—warts and all.

The impact a teacher has on future generations can't be known or measured, yet we make a difference in children's lives.

**Look deeply and see the love that makes it all worthwhile. It's a great way to spend a lifetime.**

# ACKNOWLEDGMENTS

I am indebted to the following people and wish to thank them for their great influence on my life and career in music education.

Colleagues: Mary Schumacher, cofounder of the Yellow Springs string program, and the late Ava English, of the English Trio, for twenty years of friendship and collaboration; John D. Amerman and Clair Miller, Yellow Springs High School band directors, for camaraderie and vision; Editor: Sue Bradle; Consulting Editors: the late Elizabeth A. H. Green, Professor Emeritus, University of Michigan; Oliver Edel, Professor Emeritus, University of Michigan.

Special thanks also goes to: Kathryn Stoskopf, my first orchestra conductor and mentor to this day; the late Merle Isaac, who provided score after score of playable, teachable music; the late Josef Gingold and Janos Starker, who inspired me to reach further; Mary Caporal, my teaching assistant, for believing in my dreams; Donna Brown, for typing article after article; the late Elizabeth A. H. Green, for asking questions; Oliver Edel, for sharing his gift of chamber music; Norma Cross, Himie Voxman, the late Hans Koelbel and all my music professors at the University of Iowa, for guiding me; Earl Holliday, Paul Folmer and William Amoaku, for encouraging me; Myron Kartman, Robert Klotman and Robert Culver, for pushing me; my parents, now deceased, Frank H. Strohm and Agnes Strohm, for loving me; my husband Bill and children Amy, Arthur, Wendy and Michael, for sharing my joys and frustrations on a daily basis.

Finally, my deepest appreciation to the late Alden B. Dow and the Creativity Center at Northwood Institute. This book was written during a three-month Creativity Fellowship in Midland, Michigan. There is no measuring tool invented which could tell you what I gained from Alden B. Dow and his colleagues, who freely shared their insights, their dreams and their disappointments. Northwood gave me the freedom to focus my thoughts on just one task. There I gained advice and counsel of friends and experts in my own and other fields. That advice went far beyond writing a book and the topic of music education.

# Chapter I:
# COPING WITH CONFLICT

## *"CONFLICT"*

His young, lean frame was stretched to its breaking point. His eyes, intensified by thick, rimless glasses, pierced my fragile armor. "Go in my office and stay there!" I snapped. My "office" was a small room two feet from where we were standing. It's seldom used except when privacy is paramount.

The young man was annoyed with a piece I had rehearsed that day. He had complained loudly immediately following the rehearsal. His tone of voice and body language infuriated me. I was already angry with him for other things I hadn't dealt with in the past, especially his talking during rehearsals. His words and attitude gave me the right to pounce, and pounce I did.

"Why do you think you're in here?" I asked. My face was hot, and my voice surprised me with its stridency. He waited a moment, then he spoke calmly and clearly. "You are completely unapproachable. I have tried to talk to you before, but you won't listen."

His words stung. I thought, "Me — unapproachable? Me, the most caring of the caring? Unapproachable? What is he talking about?" And yet....

Our encounter really ended with his painful and truthful statement. Oh, I went on with my "anti-snobbery" lecture, including my "building an audience" philosophy. I tossed in, "I've never asked you to play any junk, and I never will."

I know my reasons for playing that pop arrangement were valid, but my young friend won the battle that day. His words "You are unapproachable" will keep me open to students for a long, long time.

Teaching Music: The Human Experience

# COPING WITH CONFLICT

The problems teachers face on a daily basis do not disappear as the years go by. They may be slightly different, and a teacher may handle them with more ease, but they will still be there causing fatigue and frustration. Certain positive attitudes can help you cope with the conflicts that exist in most teaching situations.

**KNOW YOURSELF**

First of all, know yourself. This is hardly an original idea, but it is often easily overlooked. Before we can deal effectively with others, we have to understand what makes us tick.

Be aware of your good days and bad days. Postpone important decisions if things aren't going well. Be willing to adjust your priorities. Know your danger signs. Are you snapping at someone for no apparent reason? Maybe you forgot to eat lunch. Maybe you are overly tired.

Depressed? Who wouldn't be—look at your schedule. Look at your problems at school and home. You aren't Superman or Superwoman. Slow down. Postpone something. Juggle some dates so you can go to a movie or out to dinner.

Angry? Of course you're angry. Your music finally arrived, but the clarinet parts are missing.

Frustrated? I should hope so. How are you going to give a concert while a cheerleading clinic is going on in the same room?

Know yourself. Learn how to read the signs, plan accordingly, adjust those plans, and stay afloat. Be patient, tolerant and forgiving of yourself. That's how you treat other people, and you deserve the same "tender, loving care."

**BE FLEXIBLE**

Your greatest enemy will be the desire to stick rigidly to your prearranged plan. You must develop the ability to "bend with the wind" or "roll with the punches." This doesn't mean compromising your principles. It simply means developing a sixth sense of when to stand firm and when to bend a little. Some teachers believe that any "giving" is a sign of weakness. On the contrary, your greatest asset will be developing the reputation of someone who is willing to cooperate.

Here's an example. The track coach discovers that band contest is on the same day as the big track meet. You can work together to find a way for students to participate in both events, or you can put the kids in the middle of a power play between two adults. Talk to each other. Talk with your principal. Help each other.

## BEWARE OF GOSSIP

No matter what you do or how hard you try or how much you love your students, you will offend someone. In the best situation the person or persons you have offended will tell you how they feel, and you can deal with it. This is, unfortunately, not always the case. More often, these individuals will decide that you don't like their kid, are unfair, play favorites, or don't know anything; and then they get on the telephone. It happens everywhere. It happens to me and to my friends, and it will happen to you.

Do your best to be fair, sympathetic, caring, decent and sensitive (all those important attributes a good teacher is supposed to have); then get on with your job of educating students. The gossips, the hurts, the divisiveness go with the vulnerability of any public job. Let your performance as a teacher speak for itself.

## MISUNDERSTANDING

Misunderstanding is often caused by stress. Gossip can be dismissed, but disapproval from a friend or colleague cannot. The nature of the beast, performing before the public, makes for many possible misunderstandings. People get frustrated, fatigue takes its toll, and hateful words are spoken. This scenario can spoil a theatre production or a music festival. Talk to each other and try to avoid head-on collisions. If this doesn't work, keep the channels of communication open by using a third party who is a mutual friend. Try to find a solution or a compromise.

## BE PROFESSIONAL

Try to notify parents immediately when there is a discipline problem. Phone them at work if the situation requires prompt action. I tend to over-react sometimes, but my "gut" feeling is that it's better to err on that side than to let something go. The parents will hear about the problem, one way or the other. It is much more professional to initiate dialogue than to respond to an irate phone call.

Operate from a position of strength. You are the teacher and you are in charge. You may listen, discuss, weigh and question, but ultimately you must make the decision. Conflict is inherent in that statement.

## ORGANIZE

Organize your thinking. Learn to arrange priorities quickly and sensibly. Ask yourself what must be handled now and what can wait. Put things in writing so you can *see* the problems.

Separate the conflicts. Don't mix apples with oranges. For example, many tasks such as writing press releases, arranging rehearsal schedules, and typing out personnel lists can be sketched out weeks in advance of the activity. If you aren't sure of some details, just leave a blank space that can be filled in later. The same thing is true with making arrangements for photo sessions, a reviewer and chaperons for a field trip.

We all get caught sooner or later with too many hassles all at the last minute. Poor planning frequently results in temper tantrums on the podium, snapping at your spouse or children at home, or arguing with colleagues at work. Dealing with predictable administrative duties will free your mind to concentrate on the important task at hand—*studying and rehearsing the music.*

Develop the ability to size up the situation, compute the available information, delegate responsibility, decide on a plan, and put it into action—quickly.

**PUT IT IN WRITING**

Put important information in writing and always keep a copy. Sometimes it seems as if the amount of paper work a teacher retains is ridiculous. I certainly feel that way, especially when I'm having trouble finding something I need. All I can say is, "Keep a copy for your files." For example, once I submitted two budgets to a foundation for consideration. The question arose regarding which budget had, in fact, been approved. There was a difference of several hundred dollars between the two. I would never have been able to substantiate my claim without my file of letters.

**COMMUNICATE**

Communicate in spoken or written form with your students, colleagues, administrators and parents. The better the communication, the fewer the problems. The greater the controversy, the greater the need to communicate quickly and clearly.

This is still the hardest thing for me to do after all these years in teaching. It is easier to avoid conflict. We all tend to procrastinate and rationalize. The reasons given are familiar and not limited to the field of music education: "I didn't want to hurt her feelings," "He wouldn't understand," "She doesn't listen," "There's no point in discussing it," "Let's talk about it later." We're talking about human relations and the daily awareness of others.

**There is no way to avoid conflict if you are planning to teach in the public school system. It is a part of everyday life. The best we can hope for is to understand what's happening, keep the communication lines open, and try to avoid head-on collisions. Learn from these experiences, and you will come out with a better understanding of yourself and the people around you.**

# Chapter II:
# TRANSFUSIONS

## "THE AUDITION"

"How old are you?" the voice on the phone asked me.
"I'm pretty old...to be a student."
"HOW OLD?"
". . . Twenty-eight."
Silence
"Could you come for an audition next Saturday at 12:00?"

"Play!"
Eight bars into Fauré's Elegy, I heard a throat being cleared. I stopped playing. I heard the silence and saw the eyes.
"You have a lot of problems."
"I know. That's why I'm here. I love the cello and I can't stand my..." (I hate when tears get in the way).
Silence
"Could you come next Saturday at 12:00 for a lesson?"

I pulled into our driveway after the long trip home. "Rats! No bikes or cars. No one is home." I ran into the house just in case, but no one was there. I went outside and saw our new neighbor high up on a ladder painting his house. He was painting methodically, back and forth, back and forth. I ran over to his house and shouted "GUESS WHAT?? I've just been accepted as a student by Janos Starker! Mr. Starker accepted me as a student!!"

The man stopped painting, paused, looked at me and said, "That is the most marvelous thing I have ever heard in my life. How wonderful!"

Years later he confessed that he wasn't an expert on famous cellists, and he thought I might be just a little crazy. But he never doubted for one moment that something extraordinary had happened to me that special day.

# TRANSFUSIONS

Once you leave the comfort and safety of your music school, college or university, you will need to build your own support system. You won't have the daily contact with other music students, professors and administrators who automatically know your needs and desires. You will also want to keep in touch with what is happening in your field. For your own satisfaction, you'll wish to maintain or improve your performance level. There are several ways to get some transfusions which will help keep your enthusiasm level high.

**PROFESSIONAL ORGANIZATIONS**
First of all, join the professional organization in your area of interest. MENC (Music Educators National Conference) will keep you abreast of what's happening at the national level. You will receive the *Music Educators Journal* along with other publications as part of your membership. By joining your state music educators organization, your students will be eligible to participate in various competitions. These contests serve as important motivational tools. You will meet other directors, make friends in the field, and lay the groundwork for your professional career. This camaraderie is especially important for new teachers who will quickly discover that *their* problems are *everybody's* problems.

In addition to MENC and your state affiliations, there are dozens of other professional groups that can help you. If you are a string player and want to join a more specialized group, try the American String Teachers Association (ASTA) or the National School Orchestra Association (NSOA). Band directors will find numerous organizations available such as the National Band Association and the American School Band Directors Association. Whatever your area of concentration, there is a professional group tailor-made for your needs. They are listed in most music education periodicals, or a teacher in your area of specialization may be able to give you information.

With your membership you will receive information about conferences, clinics and workshops along with the group's magazine. These periodicals discuss numerous problems while also offering concrete suggestions and solutions. It is equally important to subscribe to a more general music magazine like *The Instrumentalist.* Here you will find helpful articles and music reviews every month plus annual features such as the "What's New in the Music Industry," "Directory of Summer Camps, Clinics and Workshops," "Marching Contests," "Marching Music Guide," "Buyer's Guide," "Survey of School Instrumental Music Budgets," "Directory of Music Organizations" and "Directory of Music Schools." Students will ask you for advice in these matters, especially regarding summer music camps and clinics. It is worth the small financial investment just in the time it will save you.

The dues may seem high, but remember that they are tax deductible. Furthermore, this membership is an important investment in your future. The music world is small and tightly knit. You will form friendships that will last a lifetime through these organizations.

## CONVENTIONS

All professional organizations hold conventions, clinics and workshops. Make it a point to attend at least one meeting every year, even if it's just a district workshop. Besides picking up some new ideas and hearing some excellent performances, you will make friends in your field.

Establishing contact with other music directors as soon as you begin your career is very important. Music teachers help each other in a multitude of ways: we loan each other music and instruments; we help our students locate good private teachers; we check on contest information, and occasionally we give exchange concerts.

Try to attend state and national music conventions. The cost can seem prohibitive, but these meetings are really therapeutic. Plan ahead so you'll have the money when convention time comes around.

Some school districts will pay part or all of the conference expenses including transportation, hotel and meals. Check with your music supervisor or principal regarding the availability of these "professional growth" funds. These conferences will lift your spirits. Your students will enjoy hearing about your experiences, and they'll respond to your renewed enthusiasm. Our music students know that after a convention my energy level and expectations of the orchestra will be noticeably higher.

In addition to the mental and emotional rejuvenation, you may also gain practical advice on teaching and rehearsal techniques. Experts give presentations covering a wide assortment of topics. The exhibitors from various publishing houses, educational institutions and business firms distribute free packets of supplies. It's helpful to gather these samples and take them home for scrutiny. For some students and teachers, the highlights of these conventions are the food samples from the various fund-raising firms. It is entirely possible to sustain oneself on samples if you don't mind a diet of pizza, pineapple, popcorn, cheese and sausage, fruit and assorted candies!

## LOCAL ORGANIZATIONS

New teachers are often concerned with the question of joining a teachers union, or association, as they are frequently called. I belong to our education association for two main reasons. The group works hard to improve the quality of education in our schools; and through direct financial help, they support educational improvements in our state and nation. I would also feel guilty accepting the benefits of their money and work without contributing something myself. I want to be a part of the shared comradeship.

Talk to other staff members at your school and see how they feel about the organization. Look into its bylaws, constitution and past record. If their main concern is protecting inadequate teachers from being dismissed, then this defeats the purpose of upgrading educational standards. Also, see what positive action they've taken in the area of pay increases, dental and medical coverage, insurance and other fringe benefits. Do they give any scholarship support to students who are entering the field of education? Ask questions. Then if you are satisfied with the quality of your association, by all means, join with your colleagues to improve the educational standards and teacher morale in your school.

**PERFORMING**

The second side of the transfusion story deals with the importance of continuing to grow as a performing musician. Once you start teaching, it is so easy to get stuck at dead center, or worse, let your playing slip. Fortunately, there are many avenues open to music teachers. You can play in a semiprofessional symphony or community band, have "gigs" in clubs, play chamber music, study privately, or sing in a church or community choir. The opportunities are there, but you'll need to take the time to investigate the possibilities in your community.

Auditions for most groups are publicly announced in the media. Call the symphony office to inquire about openings in your section. Check the Amateur Chamber Music Players, Inc. booklet for chamber music enthusiasts. For information, write to ACMP Inc., 1123 Broadway, Room 304, New York, NY 10011. Volunteer to play in the pit orchestra for your amateur theatre group. These activities will keep you playing and motivate you to practice. We all need a reason to keep working, just as much as our students do.

For twenty years I performed as cellist in a chamber music ensemble called the English Trio. Composed of violinist Mary Schumacher, pianist Ava English and myself, we rehearsed regularly with extra sessions before a performance. In addition to giving concerts, we attended workshops with artist/teachers such as Mannheim Pressler, Oliver Edel, Robert Mann and Janos Starker. I continue to give performances in small ensemble groups and as a soloist for a variety of community events. My enthusiasm and enjoyment from these experiences invariably carries over into my teaching.

Private study is very helpful if you feel you can practice regularly. Many private teachers will take an adult student on a flexible schedule. Perhaps you could take two long lessons a month, thereby avoiding the pressure of a weekly lesson. This would be very helpful if the commuting distance is great.

Many universities have a Special Student category to accommodate students with unusual circumstances. I studied at Indiana University for one year through this arrangement and found it extremely beneficial. Several of my colleagues have studied through the community or regular music division of area colleges and universities. They echo the value of such study for their own growth and enjoyment.

**Music teachers should make every effort to keep themselves active professionally.** Stay aware of opportunities and innovations in the music field by joining professional organizations, subscribing to periodicals, and attending conventions, clinics and workshops. Keep performing at a professional level by continuing to study, practice and play in public. If you do, you'll be a better, much happier, teacher.

# Chapter III:
# ADMINISTRATORS

## "THE DEAN"

We were rehearsing for our faculty recital. The dean was playing violin, I was the cellist, and our colleague was the pianist. We sounded terrible. The dean was slopping through runs and didn't seem to notice. After the rehearsal, I followed him into his office. I said, "You have got to practice. You can't appear in public sounding like that!"

I shook the whole way home. I had just insulted my boss. I was the youngest member of the faculty, and I had just cut my own throat. A few minutes after I got home, the phone rang. "Thank you," he said. "You are absolutely right."

# ADMINISTRATORS

Administrators control the destiny of your music program. When an administrative change occurs in our school district, my greatest hope is that the new person will be strong and positive. It doesn't matter how good a teacher you are, you won't have a chance with a poor principal. They control, among other things, scheduling and budgets. Scheduling involves classes, concerts, contests and trips. Budgets include instruments, music, repair, supplemental contracts, professional meetings....everything. These two items, scheduling and budgets, are the main reasons behind success or failure in many districts. Administrators also greatly influence attitudes towards the music program, community awareness of the music program, and cooperation between departments within the school (sports, arts, academics).

**CLEAR LINES OF COMMUNICATION**

I cannot overemphasize the importance of developing a clear line of communication with the administrative staff. My own teaching failures have always involved a poor working relationship with an administrator. Carefully check the protocol in your district. In a small system like ours, I feel free to discuss ideas with the counselor, the principal and the superintendent. In some systems, especially larger ones with music supervisors, not following a specific chain of command might be committing professional suicide. Check your system carefully by asking veteran teachers. Be candid with your questions and listen carefully to their advice. You may need to read between the lines. Just use common sense. Ask your administrator's advice even if you might not feel particularly comfortable with the person. You must somehow establish rapport. If you don't, your program will suffer and you will be left "spinning your wheels" when you could be advancing your program. Find a way to communicate by talking with your colleagues and friends. Your job, your happiness and your professional growth are all at stake.

**CHECK LIST FOR COMMUNICATING**

I have worked with numerous administrators over the years. I can tell you from experience that certain things have helped me maintain a consistently successful working relationship with most of them. The only times I found myself in serious trouble were when I failed to do the following things:

- Be up front, honest
- Put things in writing
- Give plenty of lead time
- Explain willingly
- Don't waste their time
- Prepare them for controversial issues
- Interrupt them if it's important
- Give them copies of press releases
- Invite them to concerts
- Be professional

Use this checklist and see if it doesn't help you through the good and the bad times. It still helps me.

**ADMINISTRATIVE RELATIONS**

Let your administrators help you grow professionally. You will want to attend conventions and workshops as well as take graduate courses. They will encourage you to take advantage of these opportunities. Get your requests in writing and substantiate your needs, long before the deadlines.

Be sure your principal and superintendent are invited to your major performances. It's important that they be aware of what you are doing. I will frequently say something like, "I know you can't make it to all these concerts, but I want you to know what's happening." They appreciate the invitation and will often make the extra effort to come. This is especially true if their own children are involved in these activities (a good point to remember when you are recruiting students).

Both our high school principal and superintendent were present in Chicago when our orchestra performed at the Mid-West National Band and Orchestra Clinic. They gave brief speeches about the school and community support for the arts in our village. Their obvious pride, along with their own commitment to the arts, came through strongly to the audience.

A good administrator is a friend who cares about you as a human being. Make the effort to develop a close working relationship with someone on the administrative staff. The music supervisor may be the easiest person for you to get to know. This is how Robert Ralston, former Supervisor of Music in the Midland, Michigan public schools, sees his role: "I consider my position as a clearinghouse for instructional information. The building administrator is the teacher's first line of communication. My job basically involves curriculum and program development. Teachers feel free to call or to come see me. They feel comfortable discussing instructional problems because I am also a teacher. Most administrators and coordinators in the curriculum division of Midland schools are required to teach as a part of their contract. It's a very good idea.

"We basically give teachers the ball and we expect them to run with it. Teachers have great flexibility to develop their own style and individual program. Naturally, we expect them to follow the curriculum guide requirements, but how they do it is their concern."

## EXPRESS YOUR CONCERNS

A few years ago, our new band director and I were checking our mail boxes. The principal had issued a schedule of all activities for the remainder of the year. The list was going home to parents, and not one concert or recital was on it. I stormed into his office, red-faced and furious, told him what I thought and stormed out. He and the band director looked at each other, probably thinking something like "temperamental woman." It didn't accomplish anything except to make me look like a fool. My colleague said he didn't think a thing about the omission because that was par for the course at his former school. "Well, it's not par for the course here," I snapped. We did get a new schedule of events, so maybe the principal agreed with my complaint. Lucky for me, he was tolerant of my behavior.

Our present principal always smiles when I harmlessly say, "I have an idea." I think he would like to run for the door, but he always listens politely. He knows that those few words spell work, planning, money, community involvement, controversy and headaches, but finally, the fulfillment of a dream.

*Good Administrators Want You to be Successful. Remember that.* If they don't, they won't stay in their job very long. Successful teachers make principals happy. Music teachers are a natural public relations tool for a school. Good press coverage helps everyone, so use this image to your advantage (see the chapter, "Working With the Press").

Here is some direct advice from two administrators regarding creativity and innovation.

Paul Folmer, former Superintendent of Schools, Yellow Springs, Ohio: "Young teachers must earn their credibility with administrators in an orderly, step-by-step fashion. Each success builds a new level of credibility while each failure slightly tarnishes it. In this way, the young teacher builds a reputation which makes him stand out from the crowd. I see one of the biggest obstacles facing all teachers is that of overcoming inertia. There are many administrators who prefer to keep the status quo. This is much easier than the alternative of allowing the freedom to try new ideas. Creative teachers must keep pushing to gain support and recognition of their ideas."

Earl Holliday, former Principal of Yellow Springs High School: "Young teachers are often afraid to suggest ideas to their principal for fear of failing. They may not get the administrator's support or if permission is granted, they may fail to succeed with the follow-through. This reluctance is a big mistake because their ideas may be quite good and are usually supported with strong enthusiasm. Their principal needs to see this evidence of creativity and initiative in the inexperienced teacher. Tell them not to get discouraged but to keep coming back with new ideas. We will listen to them."

**Think about these ideas, and then try to apply them to your school setting. Remember that parents will support a strong, high-quality music program. Satisfied parents work hard to help pass school levies. Success is determined by the level of support and communication between administrators, teachers, parents and students. Your job is to help make it work.**

# Chapter IV:
# DISCIPLINE

## *"STOP ACTING LIKE JACKASSES!"*

The trumpet players were up to their usual nonsense. The section leader had come in late, his entrance accompanied by knowing looks in the back row. His partner muttered something and they both grinned. "I'll get them before the hour is up," popped into my head. "Why can't they take music seriously, the way the others do? Why don't they care? Why do they take orchestra, anyway? Why do I put up with them? They are good kids, too. I know their families, their problems. Maybe that's the trouble. Who knows?"

Towards the end of the rehearsal they "blew" a passage, destroying a beautiful section which was approaching perfection. What was worse, they were laughing about it.

"Get out of here! Stop acting like jackasses!"

My angry words shot out. The room became silent as startled faces stared at me in disbelief.

Then I saw him. The boy who took my words to heart tried valiantly to fight back the tears. The bell rang, and everyone left except the two of us. We went outside and sat on an old wooden bench under an apple tree. It was the first time we had ever had a private conversation. "You shouldn't get so mad," he said. "You shouldn't call people names." It was so simple.

Since that day, I have never called a child a name in anger. My student taught me something important. Discipline takes time and patience and is a day-to-day expression of love.

# DISCIPLINE

The term discipline is terribly ambiguous, often meaning quite different things to different people. Many parents insist that their children take music classes for the "discipline" training. Student teachers enjoy working with our children because the youngsters are disciplined. Whatever it means, one thing is certain: you won't be able to teach your students a thing unless you have some reasonable control.

## SETTING PARAMETERS

Most of us have experienced a classroom where anarchy rules. It is an impossible learning situation. The boisterous students dominate, the quiet ones withdraw, and the rest are left somewhere in the middle. The music teacher has the added problem of a potentially incredible noise level. We simply cannot allow our music students to behave in an undisciplined, rowdy manner. We are in charge and we must not permit it.

Here are a few comments I have made to student teachers after observing their classes. "Don't take any nonsense from anybody." "Don't ever allow a student to talk to you like that, ever!" "Settle it fast. They get quiet or they leave." "Say something *good*."

As a young teacher, you will need to feel your way, see what works and what doesn't. Take the time to listen to your students and whenever possible, respond to their suggestions. *Let them help you with the inner discipline of the group.*

The exact style you use should be your own. Don't make the mistake of trying to be someone's clone. Be yourself and you will feel more natural and comfortable. Establish your own standard of student behavior as quickly as possible, but be ready to change it if it seems necessary.

**Be certain in your own mind that your rules are fair. Students can sense uncertainty immediately. Explain the rules, the reasons, the consequences for breaking them, and then enforce them. Yes, there are exceptions to any rule. Yes, you have to weigh the circumstances. Yes, sometimes you have to make an example. It all depends.**

## CAUSES OF BEHAVIOR PROBLEMS

I wish there were some absolute answers on how to handle discipline problems. I certainly haven't found any that work all the time. I can give you a list of teacher's traits that can cause behavior problems in a group:

- Poor rehearsal planning
- Missing equipment or music
- Poor choice of music (too hard or too easy)
- Ambivalence towards poor behavior
- Slow, boring speech pattern
- Too much stopping
- Too much talking
- Unclear directions
- Sloppy appearance
- Juvenile behavior

Any one of these things can trigger poor student discipline. A steady diet of this kind of rehearsal will cause your program to start a steady decline.

Discipline standards are very hard for new teachers to establish. You don't have the backlog of experience to help make snap decisions. Experienced music teachers automatically know certain things. They know that it is important to start the rehearsal as quickly as possible. Once it has started, it has to move right along. An experienced teacher will be organized, with everything needed right there close at hand. These teachers will rehearse the hardest piece early in the practice session, saving the easiest one for the very end. They will keep the students involved playing their instruments with a minimum of talking from the podium. Experienced teachers know that kids will be noisy the day before a vacation and absent-minded the day they return to school. These days are fine for sight-reading but poor for detailed, careful study.

Students need to be told clearly when their behavior is unacceptable. Don't assume that they understand subtle messages you might transmit. Simply tell them that you were displeased with their behavior and that you don't want it to happen again. It's not necessary to shout or be unreasonable. However, it is very important that you speak *directly* to the student. Don't make the mistake of sending angry comments through another child; this always creates bad feelings.

## ADDITIONAL DO'S AND DONT'S

In a well-disciplined class, there will be a balance between the need for reasonable control and the nurturing of creativity. Teachers who use fear, humiliation and cruelty to maintain discipline *destroy* creativity. They also earn the resentment and fear of their students.

Try very hard to avoid using sarcasm to embarrass students in front of their peers. I'm afraid that I've done so on occasion and have always regretted it. Students are a lot smarter than many adults care to admit. Our students don't miss a thing. When I get angry or upset, I may say something stupid. The moment the remark leaves my lips, I know that it's a mistake. When class is over, someone will point it out, politely and privately. Teachers are human and they make mistakes. Like everyone else, they have good days and bad days. Remember this and it will be easier to say, "You're right. I was out of line and I'm sorry."

# Chapter V:
# STAGE PRESENCE

## "THE PERFORMANCE"

The hot, stuffy classroom was packed with students, parents and teachers. It was that quiet moment when the judge is writing his comments for the student who just performed.

Three obviously self-conscious teenage girls appeared carrying their flutes. They were wearing the fluffiest organdy dresses I had ever seen. They paraded to the front of the room, looking uncomfortable in their shiny, new high-heeled shoes.

Their friend, in an equally fancy dress, played the piano introduction. It was obvious from the first few measures that she was in over her head; the music was much too difficult for her. However, the trio came in quite confidently, relieving some of my apprehension.

All of a sudden, the pianist butchered a short solo and burst out with a colorful, four-letter word. The snickering started. The trio might just as well have packed up their flutes and gone home.

I've forgotten their rating, but the scene is indelibly stamped on my memory.

# STAGE PRESENCE

What do we mean by the term "good stage presence"? This commonly-used phrase includes certain basic ingredients which can be seen in performances of seasoned artists.

**CONFIDENCE**
First of all, the great artist with good stage presence radiates confidence. The audience feels absolutely at ease knowing that the artist is going to perform beautifully. This impression is usually conveyed before a note of music is heard. It is evident in the way the person walks out from the wings, including the speed of the walk; the carriage of the head, shoulders and torso; the bow; the facial expressions; and the response to the conductor and the orchestra or accompanist. These gestures and body language all communicate confidence plus a sense of anticipated enjoyment and excitement.

**UNHURRIED, RELAXED MANNER**
Great artists also give the impression of being unhurried. They may tune, raise the piano bench, and get comfortable. No one can hurry them. They breathe, wipe their brow, and begin exactly when they feel ready. This unhurried sense of timing continues throughout their performance. It includes the time between phrases, movements, pieces, bows and finally, between encores.

**COMFORTABLE AUDIENCE**
Another shared quality among great artists is their capacity to make audiences feel comfortable. We don't worry about technical problems because we know the artists have mastered them. We feel confident that these soloists will measure up to our expectations. Nothing in their manner will destroy our anticipated pleasure.

The preceding characteristics are common among seasoned performers, yet each person still projects a style on stage that reflects his or her own personality. In fact, it would be ludicrous to expect different personalities to approach an audience in the same manner. I'll never forget the ease with which soprano Shirley Verrett "floated" onto stage, smiling at the audience from the wings to the center of the stage. In contrast, Janos Starker's distinguished approach to the cello podium conveyed concentration, intensity and control, first with his walk, then the positioning of the cello, the brief tuning, and the nod to his colleague. Violinist Eugene Fodor gave an energetic approach for his encore, almost facing the audience with his feet planted far

*Good stage presence also involves the correct choice of clothing, which includes the cut, material, design, flow and length.*

apart, dazzling the crowd with a Paganini Caprice. He conveyed youthful exuberance, playing with great vigor and excitement. The obvious trick for each soloist is to search until he finds the right feeling for him and then to improve and perfect it.

**ADDITIONAL INGREDIENTS**

Good stage presence also involves the correct choice in clothing. It should be comfortable with consideration given to the cut, material, design, flow and length. Visual appearance is an important part of the overall package. The artist must convey a message of "rightness" to the audience. An aesthetically poor appearance on stage will distract the audience's attention from the performance.

Teaching Music: The Human Experience

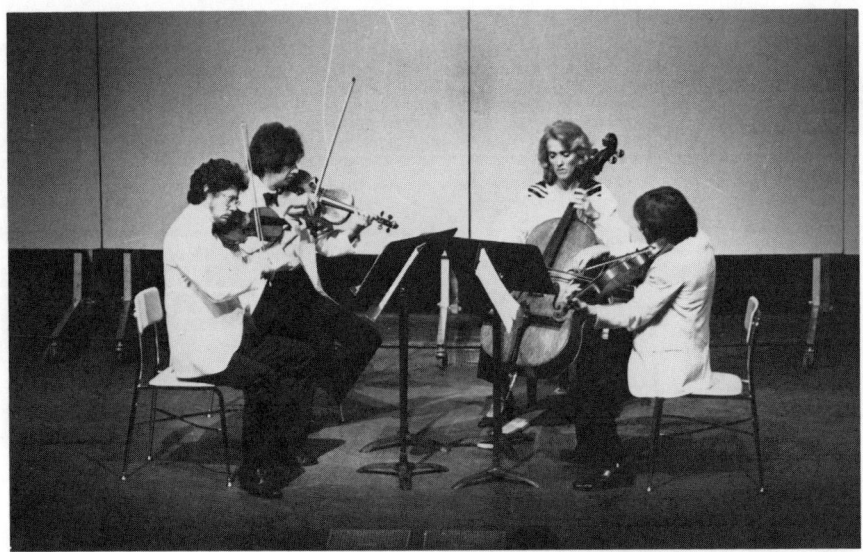

*Good stage presence is a vital part of all successful performers.*

I remember watching a symphony conductor whose shirt sleeves were too long for his tuxedo. Besides that, one of the shirt sleeve buttons had popped so the sleeve flopped around. It was very amusing, but it also spoiled the professional appearance of the orchestra. Another time, I remember noticing a young cellist on the outside row of the orchestra. Her skirt was so short and tight that the audience had quite a show during the concert. Unfortunately, she also looked ridiculous, twisting and turning, trying to get comfortable.

**CHARISMA**
Another quality to consider is the personal magnetism of the soloist, which must come across the footlights to be effective. This magnetism or charisma is elusive and very difficult to explain. It's the ability of the artist to make the listener feel a part of the music. There's a sense of "oneness" with the soloist, as if he or she were playing just for you. When this feeling is very strong, the performances last in my memory. David Oistrak's recital many years ago in Minneapolis was one such performance. The audience was silent for a moment at the end of the recital and then they jumped to their feet shouting "Bravo." The sheer beauty of the music, added to the artist's magnetism, had carried to the top rows of the balcony.

To summarize, good stage presence is a vital part of all successful performers. Some common elements are confidence, a sense of timing, technical mastery, comfortable and appealing appearance, and a magnetism that crosses the footlights. These qualities are evident in concert artists and they can and must be taught to student performers.

## TEACHING STAGE PRESENCE TO STUDENTS

Now we face the problem of introducing and teaching stage presence to our young artists. Consider the range of awareness among our students. Some children look like professionals without being told anything at all. Others, who may sing or play just as well or even better, look miserable or laughable.

As a young piano student, I remember one recital more vividly than the rest. One of the most advanced students had a memory lapse, fumbled for awhile, stopped, ran his fingers through his hair, and finally made a dramatic exit from the stage. A few months later another student, who had been impressed by the commotion caused by the older performer, tried a similar exit. The difference was that she was only ten years old, dressed in a starched organdy dress. Instead of gasping in disbelief, the audience howled with laughter, and the little girl was mortified.

**Teach children some basic rudiments, using dramatics to illustrate good and bad stage presence. Make use of the most common examples of poor stage presence, exaggerating to the extreme. You might include an entrance that is too slow or too fast, a hasty beginning, poor posture, excessive tuning, grimaces, exaggerated motion, a fast retreat and a stiff bow or curtsey. Humor is an effective teaching tool, and it will help the students develop their own styles.**

Show your students how to hold their instruments gracefully or at least comfortably, how to sit or stand, how to balance their body weight, and how to bow. One needn't grin at the audience or assume an unnatural posture. Have them practice walking on and off stage in addition to bowing, both privately and before their teachers and friends. They will feel comfortable once these basic elements of stage presence are solid and become natural.

Think for a moment of our colleagues in the arts, specifically dancers and actors. They don't just happen to give professional bows. Their bows are carefully taught and rehearsed. The audience's applause continues as long as the performers continue with their bows. Compare that image with the typical "bobbing head" and rapid retreat of so many student musicians who invariably fuss with the music on the stand during the entire applause.

Good stage presence is the ability to communicate with the audience and not let anything get in the way. We project the image of an artist by being one. It's a very important part of show business. Let's learn from our friends in dance and theatre. Teach stage presence skills, and you will see a dramatic improvement in the confidence of your young artists.

## Chapter VI:
# COUNSELOR AND FRIEND

### "DO YOU THINK I'M FAT?"

She was late for her lesson, which surprised me. Some students are chronically late, but others, well, you can almost set your watch by their appearance. She came in alone, which was also strange. She usually had one or two friends along. She stood close to me for a moment before speaking. "Shirley, do you think I'm fat?" Her face told the story. This beautiful child in a woman's body was too tall, too big, for her 6th-grade classmates. Someone had been cruel and it hurt. She fought back the tears. "Well, do you?" she persisted.

"No, I don't think you're fat at all. You just reached your height early. Your parents are both tall, so there's no way you can be tiny. You're going to be a tall woman, and you must be proud of it."

We never got to her music lesson that day. The lunch period was over before either of us realized it. I said what I felt, and it seemed to help a little.

"No, I don't think you're fat. I think you're beautiful." Now, why didn't I say that?

# COUNSELOR AND FRIEND

Music teachers are trained professionally for years in performance, theory and conducting. We feel confident about our ability to communicate these skills. Yet, we are often called upon to be much more than teachers of music. Students come to us with many problems including those relating to sex, alcohol and drug abuse. We may feel unprepared or uncertain of how to help our students. When this happens to you, don't feel that your lack of formal training in counseling limits your value to that particular student. You must be someone the youngster trusts and respects. You can help by listening in a non-threatening manner. Try to keep judgment and opinions to yourself, giving the student a chance to speak without interruption. In some cases, the problem may be so serious that you should urge him to get professional help. Often, however, the main thing students need from you is to feel that someone cares about them, someone who is trying to understand their pain.

Opportunities to help children occur daily for most of us. Yesterday, Caleb arrived right on time for his cello lesson. Expecting to see his usual smile, I was surprised to see him standing awkwardly silent, looking at the floor. His face was noticeably flushed and his eyes were red and smudged. "Caleb, what's happened?" I blurted out. "Nothin'," he said, disappearing to get his cello. "Did somebody beat you up?" I persisted. "No," came the terse reply. It was obvious that he wanted to have his lesson, so our assistant director took him into her little office. After twenty minutes of "Hot Cross Buns" and "Twinkle, Twinkle," they emerged. Caleb was wearing his old grin as he said, "Thanks, Mary. Thanks a lot." She explained what had happened. Caleb had been unjustly given an after school detention. So unjust in his opinion ("Jest for chewin' gum!") that it made him cry, which only made matters worse. "What did you say to him? How did you handle it, Mary?" "Absolutely nothing. I never said a word. He just told me what had happened and how mad it made him and that was the end of it. It was amazing. He had a great lesson after that!"

We need to teach about music, about sight-reading and note values and tonal quality. We also need to know when to wait a moment, to listen and sometimes to do *absolutely nothing*.

## TEACHERS' PETS? NOT REALLY

You've all heard about teachers' pets, I'm sure. I've never liked that term. A true "teacher's pet" is a despicable character who stays after school to earn "brownie points," "butter up the teacher," and thereby tries to improve a grade or advance in the group. A sensitive teacher should be able to detect these students immediately and send them on their way. However, music, along with the other arts, lends itself to developing close ties between teachers and students. The emotional content and aesthetic appeal of music helps this bond. The extra time spent together in rehearsals, concerts and musicals, further solidifies this relationship. Close friendships will result and will add a special quality to both your lives; but this person is quite different from the "teacher's pet."

I still maintain a close friendship with my first orchestra conductor, a friendship which started over three decades ago. I also speak with my cello teacher on the phone when I'm considering a major life decision. My college piano teacher and I correspond regularly to keep our special contact alive.

Don't be surprised when your former students bring their new wives, husbands and babies for your scrutiny and approval! It won't take very long, either. If you teach at the high school level, this may happen before your first five years of teaching are completed.

Our own former music students are scattered all over the world. We hear from many of them and keep current with their families and careers. It's one of the great joys of our profession. **Not long ago, a former student stopped by my desk, embraced me, and said, "Thanks for everything you did for me and for all of us." We chatted a while until it was time for him to leave. A younger student who had observed the scene from a short distance said, "Oh, I get it. You're always an orchestra member."**

She's right, of course. A music teacher has the privilege of being a counselor and friend to hundreds of students. Sharing their lives is what makes teaching special.

# Chapter VII:
# **FLEXIBILITY**

## *"MASTER CLASS"*

My heart was beating with his. The little boy had been asked to play a scale. "He knows that scale perfectly," I thought. "He'll be fine." But there it was—the shaky tone that string players fear. It's the tip-off to nerves, like broadcasting it to the world.

The master teacher watched and listened.

"Young man, let's talk about the quiver in your bow."

"But sir, my bow didn't quiver."

"Good. Then let's talk about the bow that didn't quiver."

# FLEXIBILITY

Flexibility is a special quality that a fine teacher either has intuitively or has developed through experience. It is the ability to bend, to change and to adapt to a variety of people and situations.

**FLEXIBILITY AND CONFLICTS**

We all know it is impossible to teach every child in exactly the same manner. We know this and yet we aren't always sure what it means. Naturally, during a rehearsal you can't change your rules for each child in the group; but after the rehearsal, flexibility comes into the picture.

Imagine this situation. You've called an extra evening rehearsal just before the big concert. A student comes up to tell you that she can't come because she has to (a) work, (b) go to church, (c) baby-sit, or (d) study for a test. You have several options. You could kick her out of band, give her a detention, or better yet, throw a temper tantrum!

If you are a flexible person, first of all you will *listen*. Listen to the reasons, weigh the variables, consider a compromise, make suggestions, and try to work something out. She could have just cut the rehearsal or lied by saying she was sick; but she wants you to know about the conflict ahead of time, and that's responsible behavior. You want to recognize and appreciate it. Besides that, any of the reasons she gave may be valid. She may work somewhere for a boss who is inflexible. There may be an important religious service that was scheduled before your rehearsal announcement. She may have to help at home with younger brothers and sisters. There might be a big chemistry test the morning after the rehearsal, and her grade may be in jeopardy.

Weigh the evidence carefully and consider a possible compromise. Could she come to part of the rehearsal and go to work or church a little later? Could she bring her kid brother with her? Could she bring her books and study in your office when she isn't needed in band? Heaven forbid such a thought, but it's possible that she may have to miss your rehearsal! Your students must feel that you care about them and understand their problems.

**Listen, weigh the variables, suggest a compromise, and try to work something out. That's all there is to it. Once you've established a reputation for being flexible, the threat of head-on collisions will almost disappear. People will know that you will listen to reason. They will not be afraid to give you bad news.**

Early in September, we send a letter to all band and orchestra members along with the music department calendar for the year. We ask that parents and students check the calendar and notify us as soon as possible if there are conflicts. Occasionally a child will miss an important concert because of a family problem or vacation. If we know ahead of time, we are able to make some adjustments within the group. We are not very flexible when the family obviously had their passports months in advance and never mentioned the upcoming trip and absence.

**FLEXIBILITY AND TEACHING METHODS**
What about flexibility in teaching methods? How do you vary the pace and the content? You may be surprised to find an enormous range of talent, ability and interest in your student ensembles, even at the high school level.

One of my favorite memories is of a young man who had been our orchestra manager for a year. He was intelligent, hard-working and cheerful. As often happens with our managers, they usually end up wanting to play an instrument. This youngster arrived for his first double bass lesson full of enthusiasm. I taught him the names of the strings and gave him a trivial slogan to help him remember them. I noticed that his lips were moving but instead of saying my slogan, he was saying a much longer sentence. He explained that he was very interested in mountain climbing, and he had just named his strings after four mountain peaks from the highest to the lowest! Then I noticed he was having some trouble reading the words on the first page. "Oh, didn't I tell you?" he said. "I'm dyslexic and have a serious reading problem. In fact, I have access to the library books for the visually impaired."

Luckily, our beginning approach uses modified Suzuki ideas, so we started the technique while I figured out what to do about the reading situation. I learned to write easier parts which he memorized. In that way he could play in the orchestra with his friends. He listened astutely to those around him and never played in a rest or past a cut-off. He succeeded because he was determined to make music a part of his life. Being flexible and varying my teaching technique simply helped him achieve his goal.

**FLEXIBILITY AND PACE**
How you pace the class to accommodate individual differences is a difficult problem because each teaching situation is so different.

In the beginning class, individual differences will emerge within the first few class meetings. Choose materials that will accommodate those predictable differences. One reason we have used the Merle Isaac *String Class Method* all these years is because Mr. Isaac provides four-part harmony early in the book. That allows the faster students to learn four parts while the slower child learns only one but learns it thoroughly.

When you give home assignments, give the basic unit to everyone and add supplementary materials for those who want more. It's a good idea to use a variety of methods and solo books. This will improve the reading skills of these highly interested students, while the variety will hold their attention. We ask our string players to buy the main method book and then borrow numerous supplemental materials from our music department library.

We will often excuse a small ensemble to practice on their own while we drill the class on some basic technique. Why should we bore more advanced students to death, teaching them something they already know? It's silly, and it also causes discipline problems. Let them work out a piece by themselves. They will be responsible if you will trust them. Let them know that it's a privilege and you expect them to be serious in the rehearsal. Ask them to perform for the rest of the class when they are ready. Our students practice in the hallway, outside, and on occasion, in the rest rooms!

Ask your principal for permission to institute an ensemble program of this type on a trial basis. The students will have to show that they can be trusted to work well without adult supervision.

The pace of a class can make or break a rehearsal. I always thought I moved pretty fast and wasted very little time in class until I visited a string teacher at the University of Michigan. This dynamic teacher never spoke a word. Granted, he was working with a small class of college students who were highly motivated and talented. Nevertheless, he taught more by demonstration and example than most of us could teach with a thousand words. He played. The students played. If it was good, he went on. If not, he repeated the example exactly the same until they were successful. Then he would slightly vary the technical problem. He slurred two notes, then four. He slurred two and separated two, then he reversed the process. He changed the fingering patterns from high to low and high to higher. He moved like a human vacuum sweeper in, out and around the players, spotting every error and correcting it immediately.

When the hour was up, although I had merely been a silent observer, I was physically and mentally exhausted. The students had learned an extraordinary amount of string teaching technique during that brief time.

You can develop considerable flexibility by practicing these few basic procedures:

- Listen to others
- Learn to compromise
- Use a variety of methods and materials
- Use pacing techniques
- Delegate student responsibility

These qualities of flexibility will contribute greatly to your effectiveness as a teacher.

# Chapter VIII:
# ATTITUDE

## "YOU'RE A GOOD TEACHER!"

The wiggly, rambunctious sixth graders were driving me up the wall, and my nerves were frazzled. "For heaven sakes," I thought, after the last child had left the room, "Can't you control six twelve-year-olds?" The noise level, the interruptions, the occasional poke with the bow—everything taken together was too much. "The next rehearsal will be different," I vowed. I'd gotten soft, spoiled by the serious, self-disciplined high school students. There was another world out there of silly, giggly, mischievous children who needed to learn how to behave during a rehearsal.

At the next rehearsal the chairs were ready, stands were in place, and the instruments tuned quickly. I set a quick, steady pace: "Ready...play" "No talking" "Three and four and" "Hurry, listen to the intro" "Ready...go."

"Wait—wait for me."
"But I can't find the page."
"I dropped my bow; I'm not ready...."
"Guess what? My rabbit had babies."
"So'd my dog."
"My Mom's gonna have a real baby."
"Know what's for lunch tomorrow? Liver."
"Oh, yuck."
"Oh, oh—time to go. My Dad's here."
"Bye, see you next week."
"Bye, bye. See you later alligator."

Jason was the last one to leave. "That was good rehearsal, Jason, I liked it alot."

"Me too," he yelled over his shoulder on his way out the door. Then he stopped. "You're a good teacher!" he said with a big grin. I stayed in a jolly mood for days, and no one could figure out why!

# ATTITUDE

"You'd better change your attitude, young lady," my mother would say, hands on her hips, glaring at me from her enormous height of five feet five inches. "Yes, Mother," I'd reply, looking at the floor, not having the faintest idea what she was talking about. I did know with absolute certainty that I had better stop doing whatever I was doing and stop it immediately!

Forty years later I am still puzzled by that elusive and evasive word, *Attitude*. We are all familiar with statements like, "She has such a great attitude," or "His attitude is terrible!" Just listen during any lunch period in a teacher's lounge and the word will undoubtedly surface. What exactly do such comments mean? What is a good or bad attitude? Why is it so important? We may be puzzled by these questions, but nevertheless, we must deal with our own and other people's attitudes. Poor attitudes will not go away, and good attitudes will help us build successful music programs. Dealing with attitudes involves:

- Understanding and building positive attitudes
- Confronting negative attitudes
- Taking risks
- Correctly reading body language and voice inflection
- Identifying and anticipating problems
- Helping others change
- Developing trust and rapport

**OUR OWN ATTITUDES**

Our own attitudes contribute considerably to our success or failure as music teachers. When things go wrong at school, I ask myself, "Is it my fault? Is it my poor attitude?" So often the problems come from my own negative outlook. When it changes, the difficulties disappear. Similarly, when things go well, I ask myself, "Why? What's different today? What's happening here?" Usually the answer is found in my own behavior—a higher energy level, positive messages and overall good mood.

For example, last semester the Dean of Music at Central State University, Wilberforce, Ohio, asked me to develop and teach a five-week mini-course in String Literature. Prior to the first class my thinking went from "I can't, I don't want to, I won't" to "I'm going to do the best I can." Being defensive and insecure was keeping me awake nights. It also made me think. I suddenly realized that chamber music had been a part of my existence for thirty-five years! By combining history, literature and listening, a short course evolved which was quite acceptable. In the process I grew professionally, extending my skills and my marketability. Poor attitudes are so often the result of defensive thinking and feelings of inadequacy. What if I had been unwilling to try? What if I had taught the class with a chip on my shoulder? The results would have been quite different, and the students would have been shortchanged.

Does this mean we have to go around with a constant smile on our faces? Do we have to talk rapidly and walk with a lively pace, eyes shining brightly, enjoying a never-ending high energy level? Of course not. As teachers we will have mood swings just as everyone else does. Some days will be difficult, downright unpleasant, and we will get through them as best we can. Trying to conceal these low points is a waste of time because students know how to read our behavior with uncanny accuracy, easily spotting phoney actions and words. Students respect teachers who act like human beings and seldom expect perfection from us.

**Just be aware that a positive word will build confidence and improve relationships. A constant diet of negative messages, on the other hand, will repel students and colleagues, making your program suffer. Find the right balance between constructive criticism and praise, and your groups will prosper.**

## WHAT IS A POSITIVE ATTITUDE?

*A Positive Attitude.* What is it? Why is it important? How can we recognize it? How does it affect us? I believe that a positive attitude is the *single most important quality* affecting learning. Students with positive attitudes show a willingness to listen and learn: an eagerness to understand; a respect for differing ideas and other people; a sense of humor; good self-esteem; a willingness to help others, to volunteer; a quick smile; sensitivity to others. The list goes on and on. People with positive attitudes are often warm, out-going people who make us feel good. They lift us up, help us see the bright side of a situation and often open doors that seem closed.

A positive attitude is a result of years of acceptance, love and encouragement. It is a gift from many people: families, teachers, ministers, scout masters and many more. Without this support and love, the child's ability to learn is limited, and these youngsters never really know why they have difficulty in school.

I reaffirm my belief that a positive attitude is the most important element in the learning process. It is extremely important to understand and to nurture the development of self-esteem and self-acceptance because it will help our students in all aspects of their education and their personal lives.

## IMPORTANCE OF ATTITUDE

The sports page of your daily newspaper reveals a great deal of information about attitudes and the important role they play in athletic competitions.

This is true at the Olympic level and in the games of your own school teams. "Then with 1:17 on the clock, Bulldog guard Gregg Ayers, the smallest player on the floor, out-leaped and out-fought everybody to grab a rebound and draw a foul. It was incredible effort, and Ayers followed through on it. He cooly meshed both free throws and it was 45-44." *Yellow Springs News*.

The team lost the game by one basket, but the message was clear. Team spirit was positive, and one young man made a tremendous effort which impressed the sports writer. Such examples are evident in all sports at every level of competition. "Was the team up for it?" "They gave up after the first quarter." "They lost when their star player was injured." "They rallied in the fourth quarter, and there was no stopping them."

How important is attitude? What role does it play? Does it affect successful performance? The answers are straightforward. Attitude is extremely important on the playing field and in the concert hall. It plays a crucial role, greatly affecting the successful performance of any individual or group activity.

## READING ATTITUDES

In order to understand attitudes correctly, we must learn how to observe and interpret a wide variety of information. A student who has a positive or good attitude demonstrates it by: attending rehearsals faithfully; being punctual; remembering his or her instrument, music, lesson time, concerts; having good body language—sitting up, looking alert, not chewing gum; trying suggestions; maintaining attention during rehearsal. The opposite side of the coin is equally obvious. A student who has a negative attitude shows it by: missing rehearsals; being tardy; forgetting his or her instrument, music lesson time, concerts; having poor body language—slouching, looking bored, chewing gum; resisting suggestions, arguing; showing poor attention during rehearsal.

Students who have positive attitudes are easier to teach, fun to work with, pleasant to be around, make faster progress, save wear and tear on teachers and greatly affect the teacher's attitude. These students will have low days, but because their normal attitude is good, these low days are taken in stride.

On the other hand, when a student with a negative attitude has a bad day, it's a disaster. There is little room for flexibility and no cushion to ease the tension. Heads clash, tempers flare, and ugly words are spoken.

Learning to read attitudes correctly will help you put your finger on the *real* problem. Words are never as accurate as facial expressions and body language in revealing feelings. Do you ever watch your students enter the rehearsal room? You can learn many things including who they like, whether they want to come, their maturity level and temperament. A host of important information is available to the teacher who looks for it.

## MISREADING ATTITUDES

Unfortunately, sometimes attitudes are completely misread. My own record is far from perfect. Once a quiet and somewhat isolated youngster came to see me immediately following his first orchestra concert. He was loaded down with his double bass, music stand, folder and bass stool. His face was red, and he was talking a mile a minute. "When's our next concert? Is it soon? That was neat!" and off he went, not wanting or needing any response from me. His comments were a complete and pleasant surprise. I didn't even think he particularly liked being in orchestra!

One student I taught was considered arrogant, when she was really just painfully shy. Another wasn't bored; he was just worn out. Is the student belligerent or troubled? Sullen? Quietly check on boy- or girl-friend breakups. Maybe there are problems at home, serious problems ranging from an approaching divorce to drug abuse. Do they forget lessons or have short attention spans? Check on the reasons. You may be surprised with the answers. Sometimes younger students are afraid to eat in the lunchroom with older students, so they "forget" and eat at the wrong period. Some children who love music pretend otherwise in front of their peers. Maybe a student won't take his or her instrument home from school. The bus driver may be making remarks about it, especially if the instrument is large. The reason given as an excuse isn't necessarily the *real* reason. Sometimes the child doesn't even know why he or she is behaving in a particular manner. Talking about it may help, but learning to read body language and expressions correctly will help even more.

## NEGATIVE ATTITUDES

Negative attitudes can destroy your music program quickly and unfortunately, often quietly. These attitudes may come from students, parents, colleagues, administrators or the music teachers themselves. Poor attitudes must be recognized and dealt with swiftly because negative feelings can spread mysteriously, fanned by rumor and innuendo, until the program is damaged beyond repair.

People who have negative attitudes have symptoms that are easily recognized. They often exhibit physical signs such as a slow walk, slumped shoulders, downcast eyes, sour facial expressions, and crossed arms. These signs speak loudly and clearly. Students are going to avoid any teacher or student who looks and acts this way very often. On the other hand, if a teacher is perceptive, these signs will tell him which students are harboring negative feelings towards the music program or the teacher.

*Reading body language is an extremely helpful tool in understanding other people's attitudes.*

    Listening to changes in the voice is also very helpful. The spoken words may say one thing, but the tone of voice and subtle inflection may show the speaker's true feelings. Facial expressions and eyes are most revealing, along with body stance and the use of the hands. Learning to put these messages together takes some practice, but the pay-off is worth it. Often the matter clears up when the true problem is recognized and discussed.

    Reading body language is an extremely helpful tool in understanding other people's attitudes. There are several excellent books on the market explaining this phenomenon in great detail. One that has especially helped me improve my ability to read attitudes and to understand other people better is *Body Language* by Allan Pease (Camel Publishing Company, Sydney, Australia).

## DEALING WITH YOUR OWN NEGATIVE ATTITUDE

On a day when your spirits are low, go for the sweep of the total work rather than a nit-picking, detailed rehearsal. Sight-read something new to hold everyone's interest. Sometimes it's wise to mention the fact that it's been a bad day, especially if it's obvious anyway. Students will respect you for being human. You don't have to give any reason. Just say, "Sorry, I've had a tough day. Let's make music." Usually before the period is over, your spirits will have lifted considerably. Your attitude is just as transparent to them as theirs is to you. Secrets are hard to keep in such a close working relationship.

One of my colleagues told me about a teacher's negative attitude and how it destroyed a successful beginning band program in his former school. My friend discovered that none of the minority students in one of his elementary schools was participating in the band program. He investigated and found that it was simply a matter of money. The parents of these children could not afford to rent or buy instruments. He spoke to some area music store owners and convinced them to loan the school some instruments, free of charge. These instruments were used at school by many children, who in turn were very successful in the band program. Some years later when the music teacher left the system, his replacement dropped the program and returned the instruments to the stores. His reason was very simple. "If the parents aren't interested enough to buy an instrument, I'm not interested enough to teach their children." Everyone lost in that situation—the teacher; the school; the parents; but most of all, the children.

## CHANGING STUDENTS' ATTITUDES

First of all, the student has to *want* to change. We have seen this happen in our family over and over. Superimposed goals come painfully slow while self-motivated goals are achieved with relative ease and enormous pride. The key lies in helping children see what is happening and letting them make the decision. It takes patience on your part because you already see the problem and *know* what has to be done to improve the situation. Wait, be patient and see what happens. If nothing changes or if things get worse, then you will have to take action. Just give your students a chance to take some risks and grow on their own.

One recent example of this occurred last fall. One of our percussionists showed talent and ability but resisted our suggestions to study privately. One day we encouraged him to audition for the Ohio Southwest Region Orchestra. He wasn't selected, but he did notice a few things. All the auditioning percussion students played mallet instruments; they carried their own sticks in a "gig bag"; and *they all studied privately*. He came back from the try-outs determined to improve his playing. He began studying with a university teacher, and he is rapidly becoming a first-rate percussionist. The big difference was that studying privately was *his* idea, not someone else's.

Last week we invited a student saxophone quartet to play some pre-concert entertainment at the upcoming Spring Concert. They had been playing quartets with their student teacher "just for fun" after school one day and impressed us with their excellent intonation and musical style. They agreed to provide some background music as the audience arrived. One of the three boys, who all happened to be freshmen, read a news item in the local paper that gave the boys' names, and said they would be performing at the concert. From then on the group began rehearsing seriously, vigorously, and at extraordinary hours. They practiced at 6:45 one school morning and for three hours one Sunday afternoon. Did the teacher demand such dedication? Not at all. The boys decided they wanted to make the best use of this opportunity to be heard by a large audience. It was *their* motivation with a little push from the newspaper item.

Sometimes little phrases will work like charms. "Do it now" or "Don't talk, just play" may be enough to get the desired results. "How can I help?" shows that you care about the student. "Go for it," "Good luck" and "Well done" all show that you are interested in their success. "Good game," "Congratulations" and "Terrific show" implies an interest in the student's other skill areas. Say something good, challenging or sympathetic to a student and you will make a friend.

Private teachers know that one way to interest a listless student is to give him a new book or piece of sheet music. Sometimes teachers will assign a piece that is too difficult because they know if the student loves it, he will practice diligently.

Attitudes can change from negative to positive through the careful selection of music. Watch it happen with your large ensembles, too. Notice what sparks the children's interest and what causes them to look bored. A positive group attitude is infectious; anything is possible when spirits are high. Ride that wave of enthusiasm and feel the excitement. Watch your top students lean forward attempting to play the difficult runs in that new piece. Learning takes place easily in such a positive environment.

**PARENTS' ATTITUDES**

Take some time to meet and talk with parents. When students drop out of our music program, there is often a lack of communication between the home and the school music teacher. On the other hand, parents of students who do well usually have good rapport with the music teacher.

When students exhibit the danger signs of forgetting music, lessons or instruments, talk to the parents or guardians. *Don't let time pass, or it may be too late.* Call the parent at home or at work, and set up a conference. Surprisingly, sometimes it is to everyone's advantage to let the child drop out. This fact has been difficult for me to accept, but there are children who really aren't interested. These youngsters often cause problems with group discipline and spirit. A frank and honest conference will make that decision easier. Sometimes instead of losing a child, you will gain a strong and supportive parent.

A student may use music as a means of getting back at parents. For example, the parents may want the child to be involved in the music program. The child resists, even though he might secretly want to participate. The child may be afraid of failing to meet the high expectations of his parents. It is easier not to try to succeed because the child knows in advance that the parents will be disappointed. The youngster may have low self-esteem and be afraid of failing. If they can't be one of the best, then they prefer not to be involved at all.

Often, there are discouraging messages transmitted to children from their parents: they don't want to spend time or money on music lessons, they may suggest that there isn't any musical talent in the family or they are too strapped financially to rent or buy an instrument. The sad thing is that the child may believe these reasons are insurmountable and never participate in their school program.

**DROPOUTS**

Occasionally I will try too hard to involve a student who has shown lukewarm interest. My efforts may include calling the parents, sending a written invitation, asking her friends to invite her to join, and so forth. In the long run this seldom works. It is correctly seen by the student as "pressure," and he or she usually resists even more. My philosophy has changed over the years from "Involve as many students as possible" to "Teach those who want to learn." The interesting result is that while our student population has decreased dramatically, the number of children in music has increased steadily. The only apparent explanation is that a positive attitude from students and teachers tends to attract more new students than any amount of advertising or recruiting. A few talented students are probably overlooked, but they might not have joined even with special attention. Some attitudes towards the music program are based on things beyond our control, making it impossible to interest everyone.

Attitudes can and do change. Sometimes the best thing to do is simply wait, putting any decision or action on hold. A negative fifteen-year-old may become a receptive, positive sixteen-year-old, with no apparent reason for the dramatic change in behavior. Accept it, and don't spend too much time or energy trying to figure it out. We change, our students change, and situations change.

## CONFRONTATION

Sometimes a poor attitude needs to be pointed out, quickly and clearly. "Look, Sally. I'm trying to help you. Why are you so sullen today?" Often students don't realize how they are behaving and what effect their negative attitude has on your relationship. Sometimes, when a youngster is made aware of his attitude, it changes miraculously. After that, all you need is just a brief reminder or even a facial expression to correct a problem.

Many teachers have difficulty in confronting individuals—students, colleagues, parents, and especially administrators. When a problem occurs, it seems easier to ignore the situation, to keep from rocking the boat. Many times I've stood by the telephone wrestling with the familiar problem—to call or not to call. If I call there's a good chance the person will be angry, perhaps even abusive. On the other hand, if I don't call, my self-respect suffers and the problem continues. So I pick up the phone, dial the number, and silently hope that no one will be home. This may seem like rather odd behavior from a seasoned veteran with plenty of battle scars. However, in talking with successful teachers in various parts of the United States, I've found this reaction to confrontation quite common. Unless educators learn to confront problems, we suffer the consequences of poor attitudes, unacceptable behavior, unfair working conditions, undisciplined rehearsals, and more. The list is interminable and wears teachers down, day by day. Confront firmly and fairly, and you will gradually build a reputation as a teacher to respect. You may be surprised to find parents thanking you for your concern and agreeing with your assessments.

Telephoning is better than nothing; but conferences are most successful when people meet face to face. Feedback, through eye contact, facial expressions, and body language is instantaneous and clear.

Teachers who trust each other share information freely and learn a great deal through open exchange. Often when one teacher has difficulty with a student, other staff members report similar problems. This approach disputes a parent's quick accusation, "You just don't like Billy." More important, sharing information helps to identify a problem and promote a quicker solution.

Trust and rapport with your administrator is important. Only by openly discussing problems and weaknesses can you grow professionally. If your administrator proves unworthy of your trust, then rely more on teaching colleagues and other friends.

My experiences at conventions, reunions, and foundation meetings reaffirm how much can be done when people feel safe to discuss problems openly. Everyone leaves these sessions full of energy, with plans to try and ideas to share at home.

Trust and rapport are just as important between teachers and students. When young people are not threatened, they are receptive to new ideas, goals, and dreams. They share more of themselves, which strengthens your friendship. Treat students the way you want your principal and colleagues to treat you. Trust will develop, making the learning environment happy and healthy.

# Chapter IX:
# MOTIVATION

## "SURPRISE, TEACHER!"

There he was, a tiny, four-year-old in short pants, white shirt, sandals and a straw hat with a ribbon down the back, ready for his violin lesson. He spoke no English and I spoke no Japanese. His mother sat on the couch ready to help. Sometimes I would correct a little mistake and ask his mother to explain it. I've often wondered what she added because he always stood up straighter and got it right immediately.

I wasn't too bad on the violin, considering that I was primarily a cellist. I did, however, have trouble memorizing all the Suzuki pieces. Before each lesson with my young charge, I would work hard to learn his next song. One day he proudly announced (in English by now), "Teacher, I have a surprise for you." He proceeded to play the next two songs in the book! His father had taught them to him as a secret present.

Luckily, my mind clicked and I said, "How wonderful! Let me play the piano with you, and you'll be all ready for the next recital." After that experience, I always stayed at least three songs ahead!

# MOTIVATION*

We are all actively involved on a daily basis in the use of motivational techniques, whether we recognize it or not. Both self-motivation and the direct motivation of others consume a great amount of time and energy, and an understanding of this phenomenon might help to better channel that amazing force in the most productive way.

When I talk about motivating students, I am primarily concerned with the students in our public school music programs, those who include music as one small part of their daily activities. We need to inspire the student who plays soccer, cheerleads, has a job after school, or always has lots of homework; and we need to challenge the student who participates mainly at the insistence of parents and who really doesn't like classical music. Now, there's the real world. This type of student must be motivated or your program will not survive. The prodigy, the gifted student, and those who have studied the

*"I have a surprise for you!"*

* ©1981 by The Instrumentalist Company. Reprinted by permission from *The Instrumentalist*, (November, 1981).

Suzuki method from an early age are usually hooked on music by the time they reach the school band or orchestra; but even they must be motivated and challenged or they can lose interest.

High-interest, self-disciplined and self-motivated students are definitely in the minority in most public school programs, including ours. If you are lucky enough to have a strong feeder system and good private teachers, your job will be easier. However, you will still have to motivate the bulk of the students yourself.

> "You practice and I'll do the dishes.
> I love to hear you play."
>
> *My Mother*
>
> "Shirley-Girl, play *Le Secret* again.
> That's my favorite song."
>
> *My Father*

These comments from the two most important people in my young life represent my earliest motivation to play music. Both parents loved to hear me play, even at the beginning stages. Think about that and contrast it with the comments many of our students hear at home: "Do you have to play out here?" "Are you still on that same song?" "Shut the door."

Some parents can be motivational masters: "Do your homework before you leave for the movie" means you must finish your homework or you can't go to the movie. Present the request in a positive way. The end result will be the same whether we say, "Do your practicing" or "Please do your practicing so we can talk about the dance."

With younger children, try to establish a practicing routine at the same time, on a daily basis. Select a time before school, after school, before or after dinner, or before bedtime. Children, like adults, are very different in their moods. Two of our youngsters were morning people, often practicing before 7:00 A.M. The other two would practice after 10:00 P.M. if they were allowed.

Parents should never disturb a child who is practicing. When the phone rings, a parent or other family member should answer it. Simply say that the person is practicing and ask for the caller's name and number. A student's concentration and momentum will be lost if a phone call is permitted during the practice session.

Have the instrument in plain sight. Cellos and basses fit nicely into corners, with their face leaning against the wall to protect the bridge. Violins and violas go well on any unused flat surface, such as a book case, piano or table top. A wise violin teacher said, "The hardest thing about practicing the violin is opening the case."

There are two obvious motivators which will give immediate results, and both merit entire chapters by themselves due to their importance in a successful program. First, a fine private teacher will motivate students to work harder, practice more, listen more carefully and perform with more confidence. Secondly, owning a high quality instrument will automatically inspire the music student to practice harder, play better and enjoy it more.

Motivational techniques will differ depending on the individual. For example, we have a violinist whose interests are similar to several of the other advanced students. He listens to music, practices his violin three hours a day, voraciously consumes reading material about music and teaches younger violin students. As a 13-year old, he is already committed to a professional career in music. His private teacher challenges him to practice more carefully, with more detailed concentration. He is encouraged to play in youth orchestras, to enter competitions and to play chamber music. He is already dedicated and will continue developing within the musical environment of our community.

The student with average interest will need individual attention, peer pressure, socializing, trips and all the other gimmicks teachers need to use if their programs are to survive and grow.

**DEVELOP GROUP PRIDE**

We have a huge sign in the music room: "Let anyone who quits striving for excellence move over for those who will not." There is an active recital and concert series throughout the school year and summer; and our bands,

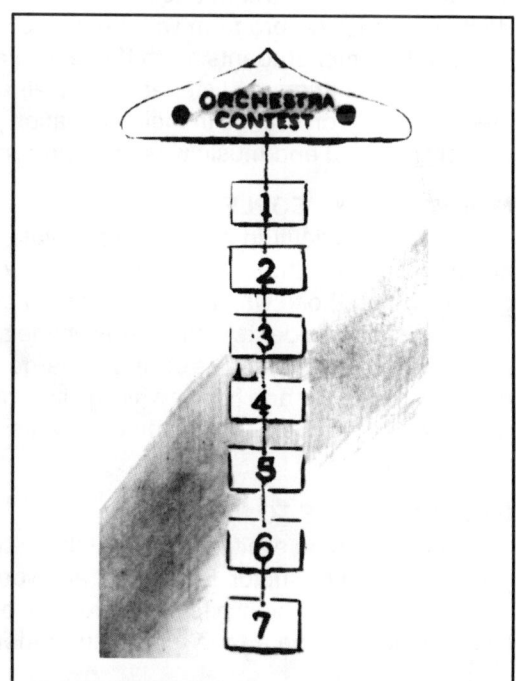

*To show the number of days remaining until contest I use a coat hanger and some cardboard, cutting off one day at a time.*

orchestras, and choruses cooperate in several public performances. Motivation and successful performance are one and the same. Our older students help our younger children while stronger players lead sectional rehearsals during the regular orchestra period (See "Students Teaching Students," *The Instrumentalist*, October 1980).* The school has developed good relations with the press so our concerts are well publicized and several articles about our program have appeared in area newspapers.

When the high school theater group performs a musical, the elementary school children color the program covers while listening to a recording of the music. Our middle school groups perform for the elementary schools. Many children play at community functions and service clubs. Performance is treated as a joy and a privilege, not as a burden. This approach builds pride, especially when the performance is well received.

Attractive ribbons are distributed to participants following the conclusion of a special concert. Tee-shirts are available and appear on a wide assortment of individuals. Our advanced students successfully compete for placement in area youth and regional symphonies. The atmosphere constantly feeds this sense of pride, self-esteem, and sharing music with others.

An atmosphere of high interest and energy will motivate your students and their parents. This sounds too simple because it is so obvious. Yet gifted students in schools without active programs can lose interest; average students in a bustling program will thrive and develop. I've had many discussions with former students, both those who are professional musicians and those who are primarily listeners. They all agree that the musical environment made the difference in their motivation. Their friends and families were actively involved and music was an important part of their daily lives.

**MOTIVATE KEY PEOPLE**

It is very difficult to personally motivate each member of a 75-80 piece ensemble. Concentrate your efforts on the leaders in each section and age group, and on those who are not receiving private instruction.

Give those students with self-discipline and high interest the privilege of rehearsing small ensembles during the large group rehearsal. This keeps the gifted student busy and happy while giving you the necessary time to drill and review with the others. Soon other students will approach you for the same opportunity.

**USE YOUR VOICE TO MOTIVATE**

Talk with some excitement about the new music you pass out or about a guest artist or conductor. Be excited and you will sound excited.

Avoid using a high pitched squeal or boring monotone in your voice. Listen to yourself on a tape recording, preferably one made at a rehearsal.

*See Chapter XI, "Teaching Gifted Students."

You may be shocked to hear how much time is wasted in unnecessary talk and how boring your voice can sound.

A performance can often become a joy or a burden depending on how it is introduced. Present information in a positive manner. Here is an example of how I anticipate my students' reactions to an announcement which is intended to motivate them. The Southwest Region Orchestra is coming up and I want a good representative group from our school to participate. It will take a whole weekend in November, costs twelve dollars, and involves serious preparation. I know I need to make it appealing and carefully avoid stressing the money or the hard work, so I give them all details of the social aspects of the event, including the luncheon, the party, and especially staying overnight with the host families. That approach appeals to my students much more than the top notch conductor, the quality of music, or overall outstanding musical experience.

Give enough information so students can quickly assess the situation and make an intelligent decision. "The Student Council would like to have a string quartet play for the Martin Luther King assembly in three weeks." The student is thinking "I want to but I don't have time to rehearse and I'm busy every day after school." The teacher offers orchestra time to prepare. "I'll coach you during lunch and the performance is during school. You will be finished in plenty of time for soccer practice. Who's interested?" Eight hands go up. Be sure to give adequate information in the verbal or written announcement, including the date, time, place, length of performance, and reward.

**SEATING FOR MOTIVATION**

Challenges for seating in the sections of the orchestra or band can be a very strong motivator for home practice, inspiring keen competition. In our orchestra we rotate seating with priority given to the older students whenever possible. It isn't completely fair because sometimes younger students who work hard are not adequately rewarded. However, the older member is busy with a multitude of activities, including a job or participation in sports as well as music. The system of rotating seating is rather arbitrary but I make every effort to share the leadership among the older students. We do not have a challenge system or orchestra test; students are encouraged to gain prestige in other ways, such as playing in area youth orchestras. Wind players are selected from those students who ask to play in the orchestra. They are doubled in *tutti* sections but not in solo passages, and are seated according to age, ability, and need. The string players will rotate seating during the year while the winds remain constant.

**FEAR AS A MOTIVATOR**

There are teachers who motivate students primarily out of fear. There is the story of a director who marched his band for two hours after homecoming because someone goofed up during the halftime presentation. It may be true that fear can be channeled into effective motivation but it suits neither my temperament nor my philosophy. For that reason, I neither use it nor recommend it to others.

**MOTIVATING PRINCIPALS AND ADMINISTRATORS**

Remember your childhood saying for spelling the word principal? "The principal is your *pal*." He is your friend and certainly wants your program to be successful. Approach all requests for money with the strong knowledge that they are reasonable, desirable, and if possible, they have always been funded in the past. For example, every year I ask my high school principal for $25 to buy tulip bulbs to make the school courtyard beautiful. This is a reasonable request, and because I ask faithfully every fall, he expects me to appear with the request. This is a simple example of course, but the approach is the same whether the need is for flowers, a $1,000 exhaust fan, or new instruments.

Put your ideas in writing so your principal or music supervisor can read them at leisure. Be brief, concise, and always include a budget. Be open and honest. Give convincing reasons to support your plan, and avoid the "tiny-whiny" approach. "I'll be so disappointed if I don't get this or that." Worse yet, never say "Well, if I don't get your support, I'll have to resign." You might just have to do that very thing. Discuss your ideas and then accept the decision gracefully.

**ASK FOR HELP**

Develop the skill of assessing a situation, deciding on the desired end result, organizing the necessary steps to achieve the goal, and then start asking for help. Many capable adults are skilled at the first three steps, but have difficulty with the final and most important ingredient. It's like carefully following the instructions for making a fantastic cake but forgetting to put it in the oven. Most successful operations, including music and athletic programs, are team efforts. The coach, the conductor, and the principal are dependent on the good will and support of others.

Do a good job of advertising your public performances. The schools need good public relations all year long, not just when the school levy is up for a vote. Most principals, superintendents, and music supervisors are willing to help you and in fact, enjoy helping. Don't be a loner, the "I can do it by myself" type. You cannot do it by yourself, believe me.

**MOTIVATION ON A DAILY BASIS**

I never hold conferences on a day designated by the school. I prefer to hold conferences, especially when there is trouble, on a daily, informal basis. Last week I was shopping in the village supermarket. During a 30-minute period, I met and spoke with at least 15 individuals, including students, former students, parents, colleagues, and friends. Without exception, the subject of motivation came up in the conversations. A former first clarinetist away at college has missed playing her instrument. We talked about several ways she might get back to it. A parent mentioned how much her child had enjoyed the group playing this summer. My colleague commented that we had better get busy with our string quartet, because the concert was coming up. I agreed and we set the rehearsal. A current student was beaming. He had just mastered "Twinkle, Twinkle" in time for the *Grand Finale* concert. Another parent told me that her son decided to give up string bass in favor of classical guitar. I assured her that he hadn't let me down. On the contrary, I was happy that he would be continuing in music and had found an instrument that he liked.

I use both direct and indirect motivational techniques, usually without thinking about which I'm using. "We are going to have a work bee and library organization party on Saturday. Those who work from 9-1 will be treated to Ha-Ha Pizza. Come if you are free." "All violinists who can play Fiocco's *Allegro* from memory will perform with the orchestra at the Mid-West Clinic in Chicago on December 16th." This statement will be accompanied by looks around the violin section. Then I follow this simple statement with a slightly exaggerated description of the Conrad Hilton's Grand Ballroom complete with huge paintings and gold chandeliers. When I get through, every violinist is thinking, "Wow, I wonder if I can get it ready by then?"

## SOME OF MY FAVORITE QUOTATIONS

The following comments give some examples of how I use motivational techniques. They work for me but they might not be right for you. Take the ideas and adapt them to your own personality and situation. All of these examples really happened, and I could write dozens more.

*Parent:* "You have to make Jimmy practice more. He never practices at home. You have to make him."

*Teacher:* "No, I can't make him practice. I'll encourage him and give assignments but I can't make him. Jimmy has to do that by himself with your help."

*Student:* Susy is so good. I wish I was that good. She is so fantastic. She practices a lot and every day too. Her parents make her practice. I wonder if I could be that good if I practiced hard?"

## Teaching Music: The Human Experience

*Two students reading the bulletin board:* "Good grief, the recital is in two weeks—I'd better practice!"

*After listening to a tape of a concert:* Wow, we were really good—I had no idea we were that good. We were really great. Wow!"

*Teacher:* "You need to practice your parts more at home."
*Student:* "Aw, I play good enough for the orchestra."
*Teacher:* "You will never play good enough for our orchestra."

*Teacher:* "Do you want to go to contest this year?"
*Student:* "We always go to contest."
*Teacher:* "We don't have to go."
*Student:* "But...it's a tradition."

Once an unruly student was banished to my office with the admonition, "If you come out of my office, you are out of the orchestra *forever.*" Fortunately she stayed in, we both cooled off, and she finished her career in good standing.

*Intermediate student:* "Do I have to play second violin? It's so boring!"
*Advanced student:* "Shirley, I'll play in the second violin section if you need me there."

*Violinist:* "I'll learn to read viola clef over the summer so I can play viola when you need extra people."

*Elementary school player:* "Heck, nobody is listening to us. They're just talking."
*Other player:* "Never mind, we're just background music and besides, we get punch and cookies."

My favorite quote came with an unexpected phone call early one Christmas morning. "Mrs. Mullins, this is Billy and my G string just broke (sniffle, sniffle) and my Grandpa wants to hear me play (sniffle, sniffle)." Guess who got out of bed, found the G string and helped Billy put it on his violin?

Here are some other favorite quotes related to motivation:
Concertmaster about to perform a Bach concerto, speaking to the first violin section: "If anyone rushes the tempo of this piece, I will personally break all five fingers of both hands."

## Teaching Music: The Human Experience

"Do It Now!"—W. Clement Stone, author of *Success Through a Positive Mental Attitude*.

There are many opportunities to instill a feeling of group pride. Here are a few direct quotes:
*Student:* "People are talking during rehearsal!"
*Teacher:* "What are you going to do about it? You are an upperclassman now. You can make a difference."

*Student:* "You shouldn't be here. You are too sick to be in school. You should go home."
*Teacher:* "Who will conduct our last rehearsal before contest if I go home? I can't let you down. Thanks for caring."
*Student:* "I'll bring you some good Jewish chicken soup." (He did.)

**FAILURE TO MOTIVATE**

When you have done everything possible to motivate a student and that student drops out of your program, do not blame yourself. You have no way of

*My teachers challenged me to grow, to think, to question. Here (at far left) I'm rehearsing under Oliver Edel, now professor emeritus, University of Michigan.*

knowing the multitude of reasons which prompted the action. It probably had very little to do with you or the music program. Walk away and put it out of your mind. You did your best. That's all you can do. The demands on your time are so great that you must give yourself to those students who want to learn.

My first year of teaching was a traumatic one. I would keep an unruly child in the group, trying to help him day after day. The others, who wanted to learn, were frustrated and angry. My colleague said, "You care so much that you don't care at all." He was right. Although his words stung and I didn't want to believe him, I've learned to put the group first and deal with individual problems on a one-to-one basis.

Involve as many children as possible, help as many as you can, and motivate them to strive for excellence.

## INSPIRATION

Try to think about the teachers who inspired you. We all had a few who stand out in our memories. What qualities did they have in common? Why do we remember them more than the others? They probably inspired us by their knowledge and examples, challenging us to grow, to think, and to question. My mentors shared an intensity, an urgency about their subject. It was serious business. Most of the teachers I remember liked me. That was important. Their attitude and approach to their work was most vital and made the crucial difference. They all inspired me and that's why I remember them.

We must motivate ourselves and our students. Through the pursuit of excellence and knowledge, we all gain self-esteem, self-worth and pride. It is our beautiful and compelling privilege.

# Chapter X:
# **CONTESTS**

## *"THE JUDGE"*

"MRS. MULLINS. COME HERE,...please." The voice boomed out like a jet on a quiet Sunday afternoon. The "please" was definitely a last-minute addition. The judge sat at the back of the crowded classroom. He looked crumpled, tired and very cross. I was scared. "What's the matter with you? Don't you know enough to have your students number their measures? This is an automatic II rating because of your mistake!"

"But we always tell our students to number their measures. We put it in writing. We remind them," I blurted out. He brushed me aside with a wave of his hand.

A gifted young violinist had performed a difficult piece flawlessly. The audience had exploded with applause. The judge's angry words were followed by an awkward silence.

My impulsive response was inexcusable. I should have protected the child, not myself. "Maybe she was sick the day we gave out the information sheet," I thought. "Perhaps she didn't hear the reminder in the warm-up room." "Are your measures numbered?" "Did you number your measures?" Everyone asked, over and over.

I haven't forgotten that lesson after all these years. You must know the rules and be sure they are followed.

Judges are people, too.

# CONTESTS

Over the years, I have observed contests from the inside and the outside, both as a teacher and as a parent. I have compared the enthusiasm and preparation for contests with that for festivals, recitals and concerts. From my experience, contests serve as top motivators, and they are definitely here to stay. Use them to help your program grow without letting them take over.

There are many contests available to public school music teachers. Most of us participate in district and state contests, which are sponsored by the state affiliates of Music Educators National Conference (MENC) or other music education organizations. These contests are held at various locations throughout a state during the school year for large performing groups and also for solos and ensembles. Large groups participating in these festivals are concert bands, orchestras (full and string), choruses, marching bands, jazz bands and drum and bugle corps.

MENC wisely allows each state to devise and implement its own contest policy. Each state's rules and regulations are based on its particular needs and interests. For example, a large, sparsely populated state will have quite different needs from a smaller, heavily populated one. This explains, for example, why some states require bands and choruses to earn a Superior (I) rating at the district level before they can enter state competition. Others, with fewer performing groups entering the contests, find this unnecessary.

Each state organization has a rules and regulation book, most have a required music list, and they all seem to have deadlines, which are enforced. Be very careful to read and understand these rules. The book may say, "You must provide three full scores for the adjudicators with each measure numbered." That's exactly what they mean, and you will be penalized for failure to comply. Ask a colleague to double check the requirements with you. This will remove any unnecessary anxiety from your mind.

## PURPOSE

**What is the purpose of going to these contests? I think the purpose should be to enhance learning, to set a goal, to prepare diligently, and finally to give forth your best effort. The true value is in the preparation and the learning that takes place along the way.**

I have several reasons for participating in district and state orchestra contest. This experience builds group cohesion and pride, it motivates and evaluates our students, and it compares our group with others. I almost forgot to mention one of the most important reasons: contest is fun, and we all enjoy going!

## SIGHT-READING

Most large group competitions require certain prepared music, usually taken from a published list, along with one piece which must be sight-read. If you study your scores, allow sufficient time for preparation, and go about the task in an organized manner, you should do very well on your prepared music. Sight-reading, however, poses some unique problems.

Sight-reading usually follows the performance of the prepared music and plays an important part in the overall rating of the group. I always consider sight-reading the *conductor's* test. First, can the teacher spot the problems; and second, can he explain them to his students, quickly and clearly. The obvious "traps" are key, meter and tempo changes; musical style; cut-offs; accidentals; repeats; and exposed solo passages. You will have approximately three minutes to locate these problems and communicate them to your group. It's very exciting and, after it's over, you may think "That was fun!"

Try to include some sight-reading as a regular part of your rehearsal routine. It's excellent training for quick thinking and serves as a good balance to the detailed and careful study of your other music.

## SOLO AND ENSEMBLE CONTEST

In our schools, the solo and ensemble contest involves a large number of students, although not as many as the large group competition. About 30% of the middle school and high school music students participate compared to 98% in band and orchestra contest. We don't screen students by ability because we want all interested students to take part.

Preparation for this contest gives the music teacher a chance to hear individual students and have contact with private teachers and pianists. It's my favorite time of year. Our music department becomes a beehive of activity, and I suspect that it is the same at most schools. Students suddenly give up their lunch period, study hall and after school dates to meet with their music friends. They also go to each others' houses in the evenings and on weekends. *Music comes first.*

It's fun to work informally with small groups. The students enjoy this aspect, too. Everyone can relax more, and we all get to know each other better.

## FINDING ACCOMPANISTS

One of your main jobs at contest time is to help locate competent accompanists for your soloists. Try asking for pianists at one of your parent meetings in the fall. You may find some accomplished musicians who are willing to help. Most piano teachers enjoy accompanying, but their busy Saturday schedules make them unavailable for contests. They might suggest some of their advanced students as possible accompanists. They may also know other adults in your town who could assist with some of the playing.

Good accompanists know how to jump ahead or back with the soloist and how to "fake" while they're skipping. They always listen to young artists and leave things out if necessary. Amateur pianists might appreciate a few shortcuts and tips. Advise them to locate the trouble spots by starting with a complete run-through. Then they should carefully and clearly mark all the key and time changes along with the accidentals. They should feel free to edit the parts by omitting difficult trills and ornaments. Long piano solo passages should be condensed unless the soloist needs the time to rest. Sometimes an easier edition can be found which will minimize the technical problems.

Remind your students to rehearse adequately with their pianists. Last minute run-throughs are never satisfactory. Student performers are often completely bewildered by the unfamiliar harmonies and rhythms. Help your students locate good accompanists. Then follow up with a check on their progress together.

You will also need to organize groups, select music, clarify rules, and coach the ensembles. When contest finally arrives, you will have one of the longest days of your life! Twice a year, we leave our school at 6:00 A.M. and return at 6:00 P.M. All of us—band and orchestra directors, private teachers, students and parents—are under enormous stress during the day.

Here are just a few of the problems we deal with at contest:
- Missing persons, music, instruments
- Instruments malfunctioning
- Ratings: delayed, lost, low
- People: judges, students, parents, pianists, other directors, room monitors, janitors, secretaries
- Scheduling
- Fatigue
- Confusion
- Crowds
- Unfamiliar buildings

**RATINGS**

Emotions will run the gamut from euphoria to despair. Some of the trauma is caused by the over-emphasis on ratings.

There are many ways to counteract this problem. One method is to give your students the option of electing "comments only" which gives them an evaluation but not a rating. We have a few students who make this choice, but most prefer to have both the comments and the rating.

The rating system in most states looks fine on paper, going from I (Superior) to V (Poor). The reality of the situation (you need only look at contest results to verify this) is that there are only two acceptable ratings for most students and teachers. A Superior (I) rating is the best. We all want it. An Excellent (II) rating is acceptable and one needn't be ashamed of it. But a Good (III) rating means trouble for everyone. It means disappointment, blame and frustration. "What happened? Whose fault was it?" But, if you read the comment sheet, you will see that a III means it was a "Good performance, but lacking in......."

You can help prevent a great deal of this confusion and disappointment. Try to help your students keep things in perspective. Remind them that a judge's comments represent one person's opinion. We hope the comments are accurate and that they will help our students. Sometimes this isn't the case. Contests can be a wonderful experience. They can reward, inspire and reinforce your students with constructive comments from competent adjudicators. Then there are judges like the one who said to a child, "Young man, if you're a Catholic, you'd better see your priest."

## ADVICE FOR STUDENTS

Here is some practical advice to share with students who are performing at solo and ensemble contest:

*Don't stand waiting nervously for the judge to finish writing the previous student's comment sheet. Tune and quietly check your scale fingerings over to one side, away from the center of attention.*

*Be very careful when you are playing your scales. If you aren't sure which scale the judge asked for, either repeat it outloud or ask him to tell you again. After all, E, B, C, and G all sound alike when you are nervous.*

*Don't play your scales too fast or too slow. If they are too fast, they will sound rushed and out of control. If they are too slow, they will seem interminable.*

*If you are a string player, the judge will be observing your bow arm, left-hand position and vibrato. For wind players, he or she will be checking your breathing, hand position and embouchure.*

*Take great care with your stage presence; body language speaks so loudly. Don't fan yourself or mop your brow. Don't make faces before, after, or during your performance. Don't shrug your shoulders when you've finished playing.*

*Watch out for unconscious negative reactions between a soloist and accompanist. This is very common at solo contest and often spoils an otherwise positive impression.*

Be sure your students hear musicians from other schools. This is such an important part of the day's activities. The two questions our students ask at solo contest every year are, "What'd you get?" and "Who's next?" We try to encourage them to hear musicians from other schools so they will hear new music, make healthy comparisons, and meet students from other districts.

**YOUNG ARTISTS' COMPETITIONS**

In addition to the large group and solo and ensemble contests, there are other opportunities available to your students. A third category of competitions involves a much smaller percent of our students, but it is extremely valuable. Area youth symphonies, women's associations, arts agencies and music clubs often sponsor young artists' or young soloists' competitions.

This category is exclusively the domain of the top music student because preparation is more demanding and the standards are very high. For example, the rules may state that a specific concerto movement must be memorized. A distinct advantage is that the judges have more time with each student. Occasionally a judge will talk with the youngster after he or she has performed. There may be money prizes, certificates and comment sheets. It is an exhilarating time for the gifted students.

The fourth and final category is the young artist competition in which the winner has the opportunity to play with a professional symphony. Only a few students attempt to reach this goal. It is viewed by the top students somewhat philosophically—the preparation and evaluation are the primary motivators rather than the prospect of winning.

Contests can be extremely valuable, and a great deal of their value will depend on how you approach them. Do your homework, prepare your students musically and psychologically, and do your best to support them in every possible way.

Contests should be just one part of your overall program. There should be a sensible balance between them and concerts, recitals, musicals and community service. It's up to you to keep that balance and make the best use of this important motivational tool.

# Chapter XI:
# TEACHING GIFTED STUDENTS

## "A GIFTED STUDENT"

    His hands were poised over the keys. I knew they were shaking because they always shake. "How can he play with nerves like that?" I wonder. But he does, and he plays beautifully. I lean back in my chair, trying to be objective.
    "How do you think my audition will go?" he asked.
    "You'll get along fine. Just play like that tomorrow. Don't get too rattled."
    The next day he came to see me. He didn't have to say anything. I knew something terrible had happened.
    "How dare you apply to this school after only two years of private study. You're wasting my time," the professor had said.
    The boy was gifted. He had started late, that's all. It happens sometimes. He also wore his long hair in a ponytail which may have offended someone.
    He was also a human being with feelings. Why didn't the teacher see that?

# TEACHING GIFTED STUDENTS

Teachers quickly discover that among their students there are some children with extraordinary gifts of intelligence, sensitivity and, in our field, musical talent. The teacher must identify them, inspire them, and sometimes leave them alone so they can sort things out for themselves.

It is usually rather easy to identify these children, although one can be fooled. They often get high grades in school, emerge as leaders at an early age, and frequently offend teachers by pointing out their mistakes. They exhibit a strong interest in some areas and sometimes act quite bored in others.

The danger is that a teacher may overlook a gifted student. He or she may be hyperactive, withdrawn, difficult or have dyslexia. If you think a child is gifted, talk with his counselor and his other teachers. Check the school files for test scores, although sometimes this data can be misleading.

Once you know who your gifted students are, the next step is to give them information about various opportunities available to them. Those self-motivated, enthusiastic youngsters will select areas of interest to them with no further encouragement needed. The others, quieter and more shy, will think about these possibilities but will need a little nudge. These students are easily recognizable because they usually linger after class but don't say anything. Ask them questions and they will respond quickly.

**AVENUES FOR GIFTED STUDENTS**

The three major areas available to gifted music students in our school are performance, composition and student teaching.

Performance is an excellent means of challenging the gifted students in your program *because it is so broad.* The possibilities include, but are not limited to, the following examples. A student may: organize a chamber music group; learn a concerto; audition for area youth symphonies, regional and all-state orchestra and band, and compete in young artist competitions in a wide geographic area. They may study conducting with our band director and conduct the band or orchestra on a concert. They may organize a Dixieland, jazz or rock group and perform at school and community functions.

Recently one of our students wanted to organize a chamber music ensemble and give a formal concert at Antioch College. It was in the spring, which is the busiest time of year in the music department. I offered to help with press releases and give them time off from orchestra to rehearse, but that was all I could do. The project wasn't making much headway. Then the father of one of the members offered to help by being the adult sponsor. He helped move equipment, arrange for the hall, and provide transportation. The students rehearsed by themselves, working hard and meeting lots of problems along the way. They needed some coaching and asked for help. Three of us, two directors and one private teacher, gave some suggestions on three different pieces so there wasn't too much of a burden on any one of us.

The concert came off as planned. It was well attended and enthusiastically received by the audience. The young man in charge was rewarded for all his hard work. He had thought of the original idea, organized the group, and then sought help when it was needed. He had dealt with all the problems of organization which included selecting the members, choosing and locating the music, scheduling rehearsals, resolving conflicts, gathering data for a press release, and designing the program. This example demonstrates one means of challenging advanced students without placing too many demands on the teacher.

*Performance is an excellent means of challenging the students in your program.*

Encourage your top students to audition for everything that comes along. The preparation is the real value of these competitions. It takes a tremendous amount of time and work to prepare and memorize a concerto movement. That time is well spent, for the student has to concentrate, perform under pressure, and learn the piece inside-out. Reward the student by letting him or her perform it with orchestral accompaniment. The student might win a young artist competition and perform as soloist with a youth or professional symphony. If that happens, take your band or orchestra to hear the performance and share in the feeling of pride.

Here's a word of caution regarding regional youth orchestras. If your top musicians play in such an orchestra, they will usually be playing very challenging music in an atmosphere where everyone is advanced and interested.

*Reward the student by letting him or her perform the concerto with orchestral accompaniment.*

The morale of your own orchestra can suffer if these youngsters then bring back a negative attitude towards their school group. Most youth orchestras require their members to play in their school ensemble unless it is impossible due to scheduling or other conflicts. This requirement is for the youth orchestra's own protection. Just imagine what would happen if they skimmed off the cream of the crop from the school orchestras, only to have those students drop out of their home ensembles. The feeder system would be cut off rather quickly, not to mention the bad feeling that would result.

I personally don't like anyone to be forced to play in our school orchestra because its spirit has always been its strength. Instead, I talk with the student and try to help him see what is happening. If the student's negative attitude should continue, I would probably suggest that he drop out of the school orchestra. This just happens to be my own philosophy. It might not be the right thing for you at all; each situation should be dealt with on an individual basis. In any case, get to know the conductors of these area youth orchestras and communicate with them. They will usually value your feedback and support.

## SEATING BY AUDITION

Most school, community and youth orchestras and bands use some form of an audition and challenge system for seating in the ensemble. This is especially true in the string section of a school orchestra where there is a need for strong leadership. Our violin teacher, Mary Schumacher, gives the following explanation to support this concept: "The traditional way of seating musicians in an orchestra, i.e., according to their ability, is the best way to get the most from the group. The first stand of each string section should have the strongest players from that section. Because of their proximity to the conductor, they will respond to his or her wishes, leading those who are sitting behind them." She continues, "A position of honor in an orchestra is both an incentive and a reward for hard work, and it brings recognition from both peers and audiences."

My own system of orchestral seating is both flexible and unorthodox. While considering the student's age, grade and playing ability, I also look for leadership potential. This may result in an older student being placed ahead of a younger one who is technically more advanced. I don't have any hard and fast rules in the area of seating placement. In fact, we frequently rotate seating during the course of the year.

As the conductor, you will have to decide what kind of seating arrangement is best for your ensemble. Many advanced students will be stimulated to a higher performance level by the competitive nature of the audition and challenge system. It therefore deserves your careful consideration.

## BAND TEST EVALUATION FORM – WINDS

NAME _____

YOUR POSSIBLE SCORE POINTS CRITERIA

| | | | |
|---|---|---|---|
| _____ | 200 | Band Music | – 1. |
| | | | 2. |
| | | | 3. |
| _____ | 100 | Tone | Strong Points |
| _____ | 75 | Intonation | |
| _____ | 75 | Rhythm | |
| _____ | 75 | Technique | Weak Points |
| _____ | 75 | Expressiveness | |
| _____ | 200 | Sight-Reading | |
| _____ | 75 | Scales | Suggestions for Improvement |
| _____ | 25 | Embouchure | |
| _____ | 50 | Articulation | |
| _____ | 50 | Volume Control | |
| _____ | (your score) | | |

The results of this band test or audition form will be used to determine seating within the concert band.

## THE PRIVATE TEACHER

**Private instruction is the backbone of any fine instrumental ensemble. We have a strong orchestra program because 50% of the high school string players study privately, some locally and some at area colleges.**

A private teacher plays an enormous role in the training of any musician. Encourage your students to study with the best private teachers available. As the school director, you can't fulfill this function by yourself. Our primary purpose is to develop the overall program. This does not leave a great deal of time for regular, individual lessons, although I try to help the children who aren't able to study privately outside the school program.

Our private teacher, Mary Schumacher, co-founder of the string program in 1964, has continued as the senior violin-viola teacher. In addition, her advanced students instruct the younger students through our apprentice program.

It is very important for school directors to have some contact with area private teachers. Our school system is so small that I see Mary at least once a week. We discuss students' progress, repertoire and possible recital dates. In fact, private teachers are allowed to teach in our building with students taking lessons during their study hall periods.

In a large system, it would be more practical for communication between the school and the private teacher to take the form of a newsletter, calendar of events, or occasional phone calls. A clear line of communication will help everyone. There may be some disagreements and problems, but a support system will also develop between the school directors and the private teachers.

## COMPOSITION

Music students in our school have composed works to be played by our band, orchestra, chamber orchestra and small chamber music groups. Our band director teaches a class in music theory which is very helpful to these composition students. We encourage them to use a number of composition and orchestration books such as *Treatise on Instrumentation* by Berlioz and Wagner. Our music department, school and public libraries all have numerous books on the subject.

We try to put our students in touch with composers in our vicinity who can help them in more detail. Our school has an unusual program called Community Experience. Through this approach, students receive instruction from adults in the community in a variety of subjects including music composition.

After the piece is completed, time is spent rehearsing the student's composition so the composer has the experience of discovering his success and failures. The latter may include poor orchestration, balance or serious technical difficulties. The student can listen, observe and make corrections on the spot. He can *hear* what he has written. He will also quickly discover the value of clean, clear manuscript copying.

Recently a gifted young man wrote a piece for chamber orchestra. It was scored for flute, clarinet, trumpet, viola, cello and bass. The combination was intriguing. Despite seemingly insurmountable problems, it was performed on the final recital of the year. We all learned a tremendous amount, including how the composer developed his ideas, what was really important to him, and how to rewrite things if need be. We also recognized the amount of work that went into the task of copying the score and parts.

This amazing feat included: the idea and its development, the working and reworking, the rehearsing, plus the need for flexibility and understanding from the performers' and the composer's viewpoints.

The audience was the final participant—an important part that should not be overlooked. When our students go to all the effort to write and produce a piece of music, it is our responsibility to give that piece a hearing. We may not always be able to perform every piece on a concert, especially if interest in composing were to grow, but we can give every composer a reading.

## STUDENTS TEACHING STUDENTS*

The third means of motivating gifted students in our music program is our student teaching program.

The term "student teacher" usually refers to a college student majoring in education, but in our orchestra program we feel that juniors and seniors in high school are capable of teaching and should be encouraged to do so. This form of instruction plays an important role in our instrumental program where over 50% of private instruction is given by these young teachers. A well-organized, properly supervised system of student teachers will improve the quality of your instrumental group and enhance morale while increasing the students' interest in music.

At first, you will have to give some time, thought, and careful preparation to this idea, and you may wonder if it is worth the trouble. I can guarantee that once the program is rolling, it will sell itself. This outline may help you get started.

- Announce the existence of a student teaching program through newspapers and also by a letter to parents. Ask parents to contact the supervising teacher for details.
- Tell the orchestra and band members that you need qualified student teachers. Those who are interested should let you know.

---

* ©1980 by The Instrumentalist Company. Reprinted by permission from *The Instrumentalist*, (October, 1980).

- Explain the duties and responsibilities of being a student teacher, either at a meeting or individually, and repeat this information in writing, with copies distributed to each prospective participant.
- Those students who are definitely interested should be assigned at least one student. After my initial phone call to the parents, the students then contact them to make all the necessary arrangements.
- The student teachers will need help dealing with several areas including music selection, motivation, discipline, performance trauma and missed lessons.
- Explain the program to professional private teachers in your area and be sure they understand that it is not intended to compete with any existing private program. Explain that your new program will become an excellent feeder system for private teachers, freeing them to spend more time with their advanced students.

We have found that this concept, which is based on Albert Schweitzer's theory of "each one, teach one," is popular with almost everyone including students, teachers, parents, directors and professional teachers.

Young children like it because they enjoy the friendship of a teenage model. Our young son always combed his hair just before his violin lesson with 11th-grade Felix. Children want to emulate an older musician in every way possible.

High school students like it for a variety of reasons. A few of the obvious ones include statements like, "I understand it better myself when I have to explain it," "Now I see why you've been telling me to get my elbow under," "It's fun," "I like the kids," "I feel important," "I'm learning so much," "I like being downtown with my friends and hearing a little kid yell, 'Hi, teacher.'"

Parents like it because lessons are relatively inexpensive; and their children enjoy them, making better and faster progress.

Private teachers like them because students usually come to them well-trained with good habits and high interest, ready to move on to a more advanced level. But they do not like to receive students who have been poorly trained with bad practice habits, so it is important that you do some supervision.

Band and orchestra conductors like it most of all. We are all so busy with only 24 hours in a day. If we can find a way to improve the quality of our musical organizations without spending a lot of money, it's worth a try.

Yellow Springs High School has a school population of 200 students in grades 9-12 with over 100 involved in music. During the 1996-97 school year, we had 10 student teachers in grades 8-12 teaching over 25 band and orchestra students. They charged either $5.00 or $6.00, depending on their experience. Almost all of these people studied privately themselves and felt free to discuss their teaching with an adult. Their students gave recitals, which meant the teachers had to send out news releases, type programs, and arrange for refreshments. My only responsibility at these recitals is to accompany at the piano. These recitals are favorites with the audiences and are appropriately billed, "Students of Students Recitals."

Lessons are given at school, in-doors or out-doors depending on the weather. Check with your administrator regarding the possibility and legality of running the program at school. This arrangement makes it easier for the conductor to offer help immediately as problems arise. Our student teachers give lessons at lunch, during study hall, after school, evenings, and weekends. Several of them prefer to teach at home, especially those who teach evenings and weekends. Our school policy says that the supervising teacher has to be present anytime lessons are given at school.

Proper placement of students is crucial. New, inexperienced teachers are never given a brand new beginning student. These children are the most difficult to teach and need the older teacher's expertise. By older, I mean a student teacher with at least one year of experience. The actual age will vary greatly. Control of placement is very important to the success of the program. Unless a child asks for a specific teacher, I try to select the best match for both student and teacher. I don't want any one high school player getting all the best students or all the slowest.

Remind the teachers that sometimes things just won't work out no matter how hard they try. It isn't a crime to admit defeat. The idea is to do what is best for the child and this may mean changing teachers.

Be sure to warn young teachers about the danger signs, what I call the "I forgot" syndrome. These commonly heard remarks, "I forgot my music," "I forgot my lesson," "I forgot to practice," frequently spell disaster. The next conversation usually goes like this: "I've decided to quit" (student). "You can't quit—you never started" (teacher).

There are a few drawbacks to this method of teaching. High school students have a bad habit of graduating, and sometimes they forget lessons, especially around Prom time. Occasionally they discover that they really don't like kids, or teaching, or both. They may have trouble communicating with parents. It can be an intimidating experience for a 16-year-old to call the parents and tell them that "Johnny is lazy." Our agreement is that they must make the initial phone call regarding the problem, and I will provide a follow-up so the parents can't ignore the situation. Dealing with these true-to-life problems is part of what makes the experience so valuable.

These teenagers need and want to be held accountable for their work. We have found that a simple, "How are things going?" reassures the student teacher that you are interested, but that you won't interfere. (There is a thin line between concern and meddling.) Do not turn inexperienced teachers loose and expect great results. Sometimes the newer teachers don't want to admit that they are having trouble, even though we talk frankly about the

*The real strength of a student teaching program is the sharing of experiences and friendships.*

various problems that are bound to occur. Usually the problems can be solved if they are confronted in time. Parents need to feel comfortable calling the supervising teacher regarding any problems. More likely, they will call to say how happy they are with the program. Parents of the student teachers are also pleased with the growth in confidence their children gain as a result of their experiences.

When I ask a person, "Would you like to student teach?", two things invariably happen. First, the face lights up like the proverbial Christmas tree, and then a furrowed brow appears along with the question, "Do you think I'm ready?" They are always proud to be asked because it means that you have confidence in them.

# Information Sheet
## Student Teaching Program
## Yellow Springs, Ohio

*Be interested in your students.* Develop this ability if it isn't intuitive.

*Be professional in your teaching.* Be on time, make good use of the lesson time, keep lessons on a regular weekly basis. Change or cancel lessons rarely.

*Communicate your wishes to pupils and parents.* Messages should be written in student's assignment book and followed up with a phone call.

*Send a letter* explaining your fees, teaching time, and place.

*Ask for help* when troubles surface. Don't be afraid to admit that things aren't going perfectly. They never will!

*Communicate with other student teachers.* You will discover that you all have the same problems.

*Present your students in recitals.* They will practice harder and feel a sense of accomplishment.

*Be cheerful.* It's not your student's fault that things went badly at school.

*Just do your best.* Don't try to be the perfect teacher.

*Build your students' confidences* but don't let bad habits go unchecked. This is a constant occupation.

*Ask for reassignment if things don't work out.* We can't all be the best teacher for every student.

*Care about your students* and let them know that you care.

*Develop your own teaching style.* Use what works best for you. Work with your personality, not against it.

*Be consistent at lessons.* Try not to vary too much with expectations and basic format.

*Be flexible.* Each child is a different human being.

*Don't take any nonsense.* You are the adult and the teacher.

*Careful.* Don't take yourself too seriously either.

*Use interesting materials* with variety.

*Ask your teacher or conductor for information* on teaching your instrument. Most teachers have a stock pile of handouts which would be very helpful and will save you time and energy.

*Enjoy yourself* and your students will pick it up immediately. Lessons do not have to be grim to be good.

*This list is just a suggested format. You will want to make up your own information sheet that suits your philosophy and teaching technique.*

The real strength and value of this opportunity for young people has as much to do with the human element as it does with music. By this I mean the give and take, the sharing of experiences and the friendships that will develop as a direct result of this communication. I have observed dozens of beautiful, touching moments over the years as well as a few that let me know my students were learning about real-life situations. I remember hearing an extremely shy violinist, who found it difficult to perform in recitals, explaining to her frightened student what it was like to perform on a program: "It makes you feel so good...afterwards." My favorite will always be a young trumpet teacher who came storming out of his room, ran down the hall yelling over his shoulder, "I can't take it any longer...." His young pupil looked at me sheepishly, smiled, and said philosophically, "Well, I guess my lesson is over for today." (By the way, the student teacher is now a music major at Ohio State University.)

Start a student teaching program, if you have never tried one, and see if it doesn't make a difference in your overall instrumental picture.

# Chapter: XII:
# RECRUITING

## "THE NEW STUDENT"

"Polly, I should have worked you harder on scales and arpeggios," I muttered, half to myself. One of my students was preparing for her audition at the Cleveland Institute. "We haven't done enough octaves in thumb position, either," I continued, flipping through her etude book.

I suddenly remembered how she had hidden behind her mother's skirts that first day several years before. I had said, "Well, I've never had a cello student this young before, but let's give it a try." The little girl with long red hair had smiled when I showed her how to carry her cello safely. "Always hide your bridge towards the inside. You never know when you might meet a fat man walking down the street."

I snapped back to reality. "Good grief—we didn't get to the broken sixths, either. I......"
Polly finally broke her silence. "Will you stop it! I can work on those things this summer. You taught me something much more important. You taught me about music."

# RECRUITING

Recruitment is the most essential part of your program. Without strong and successful recruiting, you won't have a program to worry about.

The recruitment of students for your beginning instrumental ensembles takes many forms. The most common are children's concerts, instrument exploration and the testing of students who will be eligible to start the school's instrumental program. Slightly more subtle means of recruiting include public performances, the strong reputation of performing groups at the high school level, the popularity and respect accorded the teacher-conductors, and the effect of having older siblings in the program.

As you start recruiting, keep in mind that playing music is just one part of the total package. You are offering children a feeling of belonging, pride and friendships, fun and good times, as well as a means of self-expression.

You may find yourself combating negative feelings that may be hurting your recruiting efforts. Comments like, "Aw, that's kid's stuff," "It ain't cool," "I like REAL music," clearly express one point of view. You will have to refute these attitudes with something positive. Before you can share the fun and excitement, you have to get them in the room! I always joke about the fact that I start recruiting by talking to the pregnant mother.

Recruiting means selling yourself. No matter how many ways a teacher might try to draw students into the program, the teacher as a human being is by far the most important factor. It is not, as you might think, the teacher as a fantastic musician, trained in the finest music school in the country. A 4th- or 5th-grade child isn't interested in such credentials, although her parents might be impressed. The child looks you over and thinks many thoughts. "No way, José, he's a grouch." "I heard she hit a kid last year." "My sister says that Mr. Hill yells all the time." "She's nice. I want to be in her jazz band." "I know Mr. Brown. He helped coach my little league team." "Mrs. Smith sings in our church choir. She has a nice voice and she *smiles.*"

**Students are not that concerned with knowing you were concertmaster of your university symphony orchestra; but they are aware of other people's opinions of you, your visibility in the community and your personality. These are critical factors because music is an elective in most school systems. In fact, your personality can make or break your program, especially in its early stages. You may be strict, relaxed, formal or informal; but to be successful, you *must* have the ingredients of enthusiasm, dedication and genuine interest in your students; and you must be able to smile!**

*Before you share the fun and excitement, you have to get them in the room.*

You will recruit students by being visible and by being involved. Try to get established in your community as quickly as possible. Some school systems require teachers and administrators to live in the city where they are employed. Others, like ours, do not require it and many teachers prefer to live elsewhere, preserving their privacy and in some cases, their sanity. For recruiting purposes, I strongly advise music teachers to live "where the action is." There are drawbacks, such as grocery store conferences, phone calls and unexpected visits at home. Nevertheless, an important recruiting tool is to be a real part of your community.

I couldn't possibly be aware of all the ways students have come to our program. I remember recruiting a violist because she always sat reading on the music room steps while her friend took a lesson. Sometimes I ask former students what made them start an instrument, and their answers are often surprising: "I heard you play in our kindergarten class," "You smiled at me and you let me touch your cello," "You let me conduct the orchestra when I was in the first grade, remember?" "My big brother went on lots of trips with the band and the orchestra," "My parents made me take violin, and now I'm glad they did."

## RECRUITMENT THROUGH COMMUNITY SERVICE

Our music program is intertwined with the daily life of our village. We have found that if we will serve our community, our community will serve us.

Here is a practical example of how to recruit new students through civic involvement without adding to your own workload.

Allow small ensembles to practice during your large group rehearsal. When they feel they are ready to perform publicly, listen to them and give suggestions for improvement. When a call comes requesting the concert band, orchestra or jazz band, offer the small ensemble instead. This saves you a tremendous amount of time and problems including transporting 60-75 students with their equipment. You are still honoring the request without pulling a large number of students out of class. Our small ensembles of instrumentalists and vocalists perform frequently for community events including the sidewalk sale, school festival, church services, funerals and weddings. The list is endless and changes constantly. Sometimes the students are paid a fee, or they may ask for a donation to help fund a specific school music project. Frequently, they play just for the fun of it with only a slight awareness that they are doing a volunteer service. They are also recruiting students for your program while you are home mowing the lawn.

As a teacher and community member, every time you serve on a committee, hold public office or collect for the heart association, you are recruiting.

## FORMAL METHOD

Our formal method of recruiting music students is probably typical of other schools around the country. In late May parents of all 5th graders in our public and private schools are notified by letter that the instrumental program is about to begin. The student has only to return a form signed by the parents or guardians stating their knowledge of the child's interest in participating in the instrumental program. All children in the 5th grade, including those who neglected to return the form, are allowed to try at least one instrument from each family of brass, string, woodwind and percussion.

Particularly difficult instruments like oboe, bassoon and French horn are usually requested by children with some musical background. The director may also suggest an instrument for a child on the basis of high test scores and aptitudes.

The children come in small groups of three to five during their general music class. The band director and I are situated in the same room within twelve feet of each other. We have an inviting display of trumpets, trombones, violins, cellos, clarinets, flutes, and violas. The noise level gets rather high, and the whole room takes on the atmosphere of a carnival. A classroom teacher came in one time and said, "You make this our favorite time of year," and she meant it!

The children really enjoy the hands-on experience of playing several different instruments. There is a great deal of squeaking, blatting and giggling, which is fun. It also gives them a wider range of instrument choice, and this helps develop a better balance in our beginning ensembles.

Another way to help with instrument selection is to use the *Music Aptitude Profile* by Edwin Gordon. We use the results of any testing device to reinforce the choice of a particular instrument for a child; it is never used to disqualify a student from participation in our music program. This policy is possible because we have sufficient staff for the number of students.

After the student, teacher and parents have agreed on an instrument, we explain the rental program. Usually at least two stores are invited to give presentations for both strings and winds instruments. Parents are encouraged to rent anywhere they wish with the option of having the instrument checked over by the teacher.

Children with interest but having serious financial limitations are informed of our instrument scholarship program. A few instruments are owned by our booster organizations and are available to capable, needy youngsters, free of charge.

## SUMMER BEGINNING

After an instrument is obtained, private lessons are given for five weeks in June and July. This system has worked very well with our beginners. We do make some provisions for starting children in the fall who may have been gone all summer. We try to find funds to help pay for lessons and instruments for needy students.

The public school had to drop its free summer school instruction for all subjects several years ago. All lessons are now paid for by the individual students, and the resulting teachers' salaries aren't very high. Nevertheless, we feel that the summer music program is vital to the success of our beginning instrumental training.

## TRY SOMETHING DIFFERENT

An imaginative teacher could take any story, fairy tale or comic strip (old or current) and write a script which could be used to introduce the various instrument families in recruiting sessions. The students could also act out a skit, write silly limericks, or write their own stories. Here is an example of one way to use drama to demonstrate instruments and the sounds and effects they can make. The numbers in the story indicate sound effects. the guide to these sounds follows the story. I hope you will take this simple tale and use it as a guide for your own stories. We used it with an elementary school cello choir and also with an advanced high school string orchestra. The audiences were equally diverse, including a Symphony Preview for adults and over 500 children in grades kindergarten through 7th.

## THE HAUNTED HOUSE

Once upon a time in a tiny village far, far away, two children named Amy (1) and Arthur (2) lived with their Mom (3) and their Dad (4). They were pretty happy except for one thing that really bugged them. Whenever their Mom (3) was playing her "lovey-dovey" cello (5), she ignored them. Now I mean she *really* ignored them. One evening after the dishes were done, Amy (1) and Arthur (2) had something really important to discuss with their Mom (3). Naturally, she was practicing her cello (5). (Music continues.) "Hey, Mom, can we talk to you?" asked Amy (1). "Of course, little ones." Mom replied. Art (2) said, "Mom, could we get a puppy?" "Well, Mom, *can we??*"

Art (2) said, "Mom, we're going to run away and get married and then go rob a bank!" "That's nice, dears, let's talk about it later," Mom (3) answered absentmindedly.

Well, that did it. While their Mom (3) practiced and their Dad (4) read his mystery, Amy (1) and Arthur (2) tippy-toed out of the house and RAN AWAY, "FOREVER." (Music stops.)

Now, it just happened that a storm that had been brewing all afternoon finally let go. Since they hadn't planned to run away, they hadn't brought their umbrellas or raincoats. They saw an old house standing back from the road and decided they had better seek shelter. The thunder (6) and lightning was pretty scary. It was even scarier than the old house. Village children had dubbed it "The Haunted House" because no one had lived there for years. They ran (8) up the old, creaky (7) steps. A black cat ran out from under the porch and hissed (9) at them. Amy (1) pulled hard on the front door. It slowly creaked open (7) and then mysteriously (10) slammed shut (11). They were all alone. . .(12) they hoped.

Their knees were knocking (13) and their hearts were pounding. "Shhh," said Art (2), "We might wake somebody up." Amy (1) said, "Who? Nobody lives here, you silly!" After all, she was ten years old and Art was only six.

The rain went from a few drops on the roof (14) to a flood (15) in a few seconds. Something went scampering across the roof (16), a squirrel, probably. Then an owl (17) hooted and some wild animal howled (18). The children were cold and hungry. "Let's snoop around," Art (2) whispered. "Might as well." Holding hands and moving very slowly, they inched their way across the big room. Then they stopped. "What's that?" said Amy (1). (19) "Oh, it's just some rats in the wallboard. . .I think." "What's that?" Art asked (2). (20) "Not to worry, it's just the wind whistling in the trees." They went a little further. The thunder (6) and lightning were closer now. They pushed another door open (7) and went further. They heard footsteps (21) upstairs, followed by a blood-curdling scream (22). They ran through the room, pushed open the door (7), raced down the creaky steps (7), didn't even hear the cat hiss (9) or the owl hoot (17) or the wind (20) or the rain.

They ran home as fast as their legs would carry them. They were sure that their mom (3) would still be practicing her cello, and their daddy (4) would still be reading his mystery. Instead, they were both looking out the window. They hugged their soaking wet children as they ran inside saying, "Yes, yes, you may each have a puppy and don't ever, ever run away from home again!"

And they never did. . . .

THE END (23)

**SOUND EFFECTS: CELLO CHOIR**

(1) Amy: very high trill
(2) Arthur: gliss up and down on G string
(3) Mom: busy tremolo between two medium high notes
(4) Dad: D♭ to open C, slowly followed by a snore & whistle
(5) Bocherrini's Minuet
(6) Thunder: low rumble with tremolo
(7) Creaky steps: pull bow slowly, close to bridge with lots of pressure
(8) Fast footsteps: rapid knocking on front or side of cello
(9) Cat hissing: harmonics, up high, sliding or voice hiss
(10) Mysterious sound: glissandos up high or down low
(11) Slammed door: loud knock on back of cello
(12) Hee, hee: high harmonic
(13) Knees knocking: knock on cello
(14) Raindrops, few: one person slowly knocks on cello with knuckles (or Col Legno)
(15) Raindrops, many: all cellos knock rapidly on cello with knuckles (or Col Legno)
(16) Squirrel scampering: half steps, fast with single bows, high
(17) Owl: minor third, up high, dropping off or use voice
(18) Animal howling: glissando downwards, lower or use voice
(19) Rat gnawing: slow bow, close to bridge of G string
(20) Wind whistling: fast, high harmonic glissandos
(21) Footstep, getting nearer: knocking on back of cello starting softer and increasing
(22) Scream: high note, pressed hard or hard, fast bow stroke
(23) The End: G and C, followed by bow

*Recruitment is the most essential part of your program. Your primary task is to keep those new faces coming.*

The possibilities for incorporating writing, drama, dance and mime with your music classes are endless. Use this idea as a recruiting tool or to add variety to a concert. the audiences and performers will enjoy something different. Remember that our primary task is to keep those new faces coming every year.

# Chapter XIII:
# **FUNDING**

## "THE FELLOWSHIP"

The sky has been changing colors and cloud formations during our dinner. The pine trees surrounding the veranda are making a music of their own. The wind is just enough to start them singing. Noisy birds are calling to each other and to us. Wild flowers sit quietly among the ferns and seedlings. Two squirrels are quarreling in the brush nearby.

Our table is full of good things to eat: a fruit platter piled high with apples, melons and berries surrounded by cheese and crisp crackers. White wine, napkins and silverware add a touch of elegance.

The moon appears and we realize it has grown dark while we discussed life, religion and the creative process. We know we are lucky. We are almost embarrassed by our good fortune.

"Well, don't forget, kiddo, we applied for this fellowship," my friend tossed out for comment.

She's right, you know. To receive, you have to ask. So ask.

# FUNDING

One of your biggest headaches will be the constant problem of raising funds. Music programs usually require considerable financial support beyond what the school district can provide. The stronger the program, the greater the need for additional funds. There is one simple way to avoid money worries: don't do anything special or exciting! The minute you go beyond daily rehearsals and two or three concerts a year, you will find yourself needing funds.

There are at least three sources of revenue available to support the goals of the music teacher. First, the school system usually provides the teachers' salaries, along with the purchase of basic items such as sheet music and equipment. School districts may buy instruments for the band or orchestra, but this is not always the case especially in smaller school systems.

## BOOSTER CLUBS

Second, a booster club will be needed for almost anything beyond basic expenses. In our school-community program, that includes instruments, lesson scholarships, travel, sheet music and teacher's supplemental fees. In schools with marching band programs, a considerable responsibility will be the cost of travel and the purchase and maintenance of uniforms.

You are very fortunate if you work where a strong support group already exists. Your main job will be to keep the members clearly informed of your needs and priorities. You will have to go to meetings and sell your ideas. These clubs may be very informal, meeting only once a year to raise money for a specific task. For example, our band parents used to run a Band Fair every fall. This was a popular community event with games, dunking machines, terrific food and continuous music. The approximately $1,500.00 raised at the fair was an important supplement to the band's school budget. Unfortunately, the advent of two-career families and a smaller pool of volunteers has eliminated this activity for the time being.

A more formal organization, the Yellow Springs Youth Orchestra Association, Inc., meets year 'round and provides extensive support for the orchestra program. It is incorporated as a non-profit group which makes it eligible to seek state, federal and private foundation funding. Its current annual budget is just under $10,000.00

The important thing to remember about booster clubs is that their function is one of support. They are in existence to help you, and while they are not in a position to dictate policy, they will lend support in areas other than funding, if you request it. Booster clubs have been known to save music programs in danger of being eliminated.

## TRAVEL

Travel is an example of a special project which may concern you quite early in your career. It can be a major financial concern for performing groups. To minimize this cost, we have taken short, inexpensive trips to area universities using school buses for transportation. We have also traveled longer distances using commercial carriers. But the strain of raising the required large sums of money has to be considered carefully. Try to weigh the expenditure of energy against the value gained. In doing so, your on-going program should be the *most* important consideration.

If your community can also support travel, by all means include it in your activities. Trips help develop group unity and community pride. The educational value of travel should be obvious, but it includes some things that might not be noticed, such as navigating one's way through a large airport or hotel. We always include time for sightseeing when we visit large cities. Many of our students gain experiences which would only be possible through these group excursions. The administrative team supports these trips, especially when we appear at music conventions. They provide chaperons, arrange release time from school, and give strong moral support. Administrators also frequently attend these special performances, along with representatives from the boosters' clubs and parents.

## BASIC NEEDS

Sometimes you will need to raise money for basic needs as well as for special projects. Here are two examples to illustrate this point.

Our music students give recitals during the year which include chamber music and solos by vocalists and instrumentalists. In addition, local piano teachers, the community chorus and theatre groups all use the music room for rehearsal and programs. Yet, for several years we were without a decent piano. By pooling our community resources, the orchestra boosters mounted a campaign to buy a quality instrument. The music students helped by selling cheese and sausage, our school forest organization donated $1,400.00, and an orchestra family sent a check for $1,000.00. It was hard work, but the task was successfully completed. Now, all the groups who use the high school music room enjoy a beautiful instrument which the schools were simply unable to provide.

We had to do the same thing to get an exhaust fan for the rehearsal room. We would practically die from the heat in the early fall and late spring. We had the choice of waiting another few years until school funds appeared, or we could raise the money and breathe. It's not very exciting trying to raise money for an exhaust fan — people would much rather donate money for a trip to Europe!

**One day, I found myself worrying about some fund raising project the orchestra was conducting. "I spend more time raising money than I do studying my scores," I thought. Then I realized something. It's not all that different from what community and professional orchestras do everywhere. In fact, in one way or another, musicians have always had to be concerned with beauty and art on the one hand and feeding the family on the other.**

Early in my teaching career, I had the idea that it would be fun and interesting for our orchestra to visit a major university. We made the necessary arrangements, chartered the buses, and started raising the money. I was chatting with our school counselor's volunteer secretary when the phone rang. The message was terribly disappointing. Somehow the bus company had a new employee who had made a serious error in quoting our prices to the tune of $600.00 short! I hung up the phone and burst into tears. There was no way in the world we could come up with $600.00 extra. We were barely going to make it at the quoted price.

My friend said, "Just a minute, young lady. It's silly to get all upset!" She picked up the phone, called a colleague, and said, "We have a little problem to solve. Could you send over a check for $600.00, please?" My eyes must have bulged out of my head! My friend just happened to be an extremely wealthy "volunteer." Lucky for us, I was at the right place at the right time. It doesn't usually happen that way.

Our money problems aren't usually solved by guardian angels. They tend to be worked out through committees, cheese and sausage drives, donations, bake sales, ticket campaigns — less exciting but more reliable methods.

Fund raising occupies a large percent of most volunteer organizations' time. It gives adults an excuse to get together in the evening, drink coffee and eat cookies, while supporting worthwhile projects. Our village has to have more meetings on any given night than any town its size in the country.

A friend of mine went to a meeting one evening. The host took her coat, ushered her into the living room, which was crowded with bright, articulate people who were all drinking coffee and eating cookies. She was at the meeting for 45 minutes before she realized that she was at the wrong house and the wrong meeting! The topics of discussion for those 45 minutes had been fund raising, the very subject she was expecting to discuss!

Working together for a common cause is what it's all about. The goal, whether it's new uniforms or a trip to the Rose Bowl, must be clearly defined, explained and justified. Someone with organizational skills needs to devise a plan, with input from many other people. Once the course is set and jobs are assigned, the momentum starts to build. The planning stages of these drives can be frustrating because they take considerable time and energy while you are trying to be patient. Trust these good people, and they will usually come through, working hard and enjoying their involvement.

**FOUNDATION FUNDS**

A third source of funding is available through state and private foundations. Many foundations are interested in funding educational projects.

My first appearance before a local foundation board was rather routine, although I was quite nervous about the meeting. I needed money to have a brochure printed about our orchestra program. People were requesting materials and I thought that a simple, inexpensive brochure would be the answer. It wasn't a great idea, but it was practical and it only cost $150.00. The foundation board was polite, the members asked some questions, and in the end, gave me the money. Still, something didn't feel quite right. Just as I was leaving the room, the president said, "Bring us a better idea next time and ask for more money. This wasn't much fun!"

I think I know what he meant by his comment. I should have been able to raise $150.00 somewhere else, perhaps through the boosters' club or in private donations. Foundations are interested in *ideas, exciting* and *innovative ideas*. I found that fact very interesting and it was substantiated by other foundations. The amount of money is seldom the primary concern.

**GUIDE TO GRANT WRITING**

Here is a brief formula for grant writing which may help you get started.

Your first job is to get an idea. Think of something you would like to do that requires funding. It needs to be interesting, innovative and unique. You also have to show some evidence that it has a strong possibility for success. After the idea is clear in your mind, put it on paper. Scrutinize the idea. Is it interesting and unique? Is it feasible?

The next step is to locate foundations that fund this kind of project. Go to the library and check several sources. *The National Directory of Grants and Aid to Individuals in the Arts, Grants for the Arts* by Virginia White and the *Complete Grants Sourcebook for Higher Education* are good examples. Write to those foundations which seem most likely to fit your needs, requesting an application blank and additional information. When it arrives, read this information very carefully, underlining the important points. The application procedure may include suggestions for budget development, the number of recommendations and of prime concern, the deadlines.

Your proposal needs to be written in a concise manner and should be professionally typed. If letters of recommendation are required, seek recognized authorities who are familiar with your work. Be sure to carefully observe all instructions, *especially the deadlines.*

If your proposal is rejected, try to find out why. Some foundations will share this information with you while others will simply send you a form letter. If you believe your basic idea is good, rewrite the proposal and submit it to a different funding agency. In the grant writing business, persistence pays.

You will need to spend considerable time and thought developing all areas of funding. The school budget should include as many of the necessities as possible. Work with your building principal to see if this budget could be expanded. That will leave the boosters' clubs with the responsibility of providing for extras such as uniforms and travel. Foundations can be tapped for those special projects that are the "icing on the cake." They may not be basic to the success of your program, but they add that extra prestige and excitement. I have found it necessary to attack the funding problem on all fronts to keep a successful program operating.

# Chapter XIV: WORKING WITH THE PRESS

## "EDITORS"

*"Please tell your readers that we are human beings, too. We are under tremendous pressures that are aggravated by living in a goldfish bowl. We may sound grumpy over the phone because your call may have been the fifth interruption in ten minutes. Be a little sympathetic to our problems."*

                                  **John Palen, editor**
                                  **Midland Daily News (Michigan)**

*"A reader could follow all the advice in your media chapter, and we still might not print their news. We print your news because people read it. They read it because their children (relatives, friends) are involved and are excited. In other words, good public relations is important but it's just a part of the total picture. Bring us news that is interesting so we know that people will read it. This is a self-perpetuating cycle and a very successful one."*

                                    **Don Wallis, editor**
                                  **Yellow Springs News (Ohio)**

# WORKING WITH THE PRESS

"I'd much rather look at your face than at your press release!" quipped the veteran editor. We were enjoying a brief chat during my annual visit to Interlochen's National Music Camp. Over the years, he taught me a great deal about the human side of good press relations. I'd like to encourage all music teachers to investigate this important area. It can help your program develop much broader community support.

Many people feel that newspapers are simply not interested in news about school activities. This may be true where you live and work. It just means that you'll have to build that interest by doing a strong selling job.

The Interlochen editor was joking a little, but his message was still very clear. Newspaper people are human, and they enjoy the personal touch. Now, if you stopped to chat just before deadline, your reception would be anything but cordial!

Go meet the people who will most likely be interested in reading your material. Depending on the size of the paper, you might be talking to a fine arts editor, school news or community service writer, or in some cases, the main editor. Tell them about your program, and give them some written information such as an overview of the concert calendar. The main purpose of this visit is just to get acquainted.

## PRESS RELEASES

Your next step will be to start sending news releases and photographs, well in advance of an upcoming activity. If the event is very special and you especially need good coverage, call the person who will be receiving the release. That way he'll notice your letter when it arrives, making it less likely to end up in the waste basket.

**"Less is Best" is my motto when I'm writing press releases. Unless you have to work through a public relations official in your school, I suggest that you always write the releases yourself. For one thing, you know all the information, and you know what facts should be emphasized.** The release should contain the following information in the first paragraph: tell your readers Who, What, When, Where and Why, along with the ticket prices. Try to make it interesting by including anything that is unusual or special about the concert.

Write in a concise manner, preferably on one page, typed and double-spaced. Always include your name, title and phone number at the top of the page. It's helpful to list both your school and home phone numbers. If the editor wants to talk to you, he wants to do it immediately.

You should be able to write an interesting release in less than an hour. After it's written, ask other people to help with the typing, addressing envelopes and mailing. Compared to the long hours spent in preparing the concert, this hour is a wise investment.

There are some important questions you need to ask your own newspaper staff. Find out what size and type of photographs they prefer. Some general suggestions I've been given are that close-ups are best, always use black and white film, and try for candid action shots rather than posed shots.

Be sure to ask about the correct timing of your releases. If it arrives too early, it may be misplaced or overlooked. If it arrives too late, it will automatically be tossed out. The editor or office manager can tell you exactly how much lead time is needed.

Once you've established solid contacts at the newspaper office, keep them positive. Take the time to say "thanks" for their coverage. Work hard to meet their deadlines. Don't waste time complaining about mistakes; simply ask for a correction in the next issue.

*Newspapers like to use action photos rather than posed shots.*

Good press helps to build pride within your group. It also gives parents a chance to enjoy reading about their children's activities, and other members of the community who may not attend the concerts will faithfully follow the announcements and reviews. Positive press about one department in your school can also help the school's overall image.

If you would like to have more information about how to write a release, there is an excellent source available. Contact Marcus L. Neiman, Fine Arts Consultant for the Medina County Schools Educational Service Center at 124 West Washington Street, Medina, Ohio 44256 (phone: 330-723-6393; FAX: 330-722-9206). His packet of handouts includes *Building Bridges of Understanding: Public/Community Relations for Music Educators* and includes several excellent examples of press coverage for school music ensembles. His information is practical, concise and extremely helpful.

In summary, good press and public relations will help your music program develop broader community support and interest. Take the initiative and the time to establish personal contact with your area newspapers. Send concise, well-written releases with photographs, always allowing sufficient lead time. Maintain this personal contact with occasional letters and phone calls. Remember to appreciate their support and treat the newspaper staff with courtesy.

# Chapter XV:
# A SHOESTRING ARTIST SERIES

## "GUEST ARTISTS"

Our guest artists were playing on stage, deeply involved in their music. I was standing at the back of the room, entranced. Suddenly I saw a little wiggly boy in the front row, talking to his friend. His parents were "miles away" on the other side of the room. I knew what would happen if the violinist noticed him. "Instant mincemeat," I thought. "Little boys, or girls for that matter, do not sit in the front row at concerts and talk. No, No, No!"

It took about thirty seconds. Dressed in a red evening gown, I flowed down one aisle, picked up the child, flowed out the other, continuing into the outer hallway, never missing a beat. The child was so surprised that he didn't make a sound. He just looked at me with those enormous eyes and long eyelashes. If the audience had blinked, they would have missed it.

After the concert, the violinist stood talking to someone in the receiving line. "It was the strangest thing. Right in the middle of the Kodaly, I thought I saw a flash of red pass before my eyes!" His friend laughed and winked at me but never said a word!

# A SHOESTRING ARTIST SERIES

You might be surprised to learn that it is quite possible to run an informal concert series with very little money. Guest soloists may be willing to visit your school, free of charge, if you plan ahead.

We have found that artists enjoy visiting in a relaxed atmosphere. For example, we had a potluck supper for pianist Roosevelt Newson just before his "informance," the term for his presentation (an informal, informative performance). People were friendly, everyone had a good time, and our students had the opportunity to become personally acquainted with a concert pianist. For Mr. Newson it was a pleasant change from restaurant meals, airports and cabs. An artist once said to me, "I'll be in Venice next week at this time." "How wonderful; I wish I could see Venice." "So do I," was the frank reply. "I'll see the inside of a cab, a hotel and a concert hall."

**CONTACT YOUR AREA SYMPHONY**

If you are interested in starting an artist series, your first step is to contact your area symphony office. Check to see which concert artists will be engaged for two concerts on consecutive nights. That simply means there should be some free time during the day when the soloist isn't rehearsing with the orchestra, practicing by himself, or catching up on some rest. This is especially true if the orchestra is semi-professional and rehearses only in the evening. We have had artists come on the spur of the moment when the orchestra manager suggested it.

**Occasionally, the artist will request the opportunity to give a master class at a nearby school. Word will get around among the symphony managers that your school is available for this kind of impromptu visit. The reception you give visiting artists will make an important impression. Make them feel welcome, just as you would guests in your own home.**

Sometimes it's not possible for the artist to visit your school, even if he would like to. In this case, ask permission to attend a dress rehearsal and go backstage at the performance. We take a group to hear the Dayton Philharmonic series, and the students especially enjoy this aspect of the program. Sometimes we take gifts or flowers, which add to the festivity of the occasion.

Concert artists frequently return to the same orchestra, especially if the concert was a tremendous success. They may remember the name of your school and ask to visit during their next engagement.

Keep in mind that concert artists lead hectic, demanding lives. They may be willing to spend some time with your students just because they want something different to do. The exposure is also very important for their careers. Concert artists are aware that exposure and re-engagements are the life blood of the business. The receiving line, the "concert after the concert," and even the visits to schools are all part of the life of a concert artist.

Here is an example of the kind of interaction I mean, written as a press release.

*"I can't see the faces or anything else beyond the footlights."*

# PIANIST ROOSEVELT NEWSON
# A GIFTED MUSICIAN VISITS THE HIGH SCHOOL

A young man with a winning smile and a musical gift spent two hours at Yellow Springs High School last Thursday evening. Roosevelt Newson, concert pianist and speaker, gave an "in-formance," an informal, informative performance and his program was most enjoyable, sparkling with wit and spontaneity.

We heard Aaron Copland's "The Cat and the Mouse." He asked, "Did the cat catch the mouse or not?" The audience was divided, but the answer was absolutely "YES." Mr. Copland had written the fatal word at the end of his score. Mr. Newson played a beautiful Brahms Intermezzo ("I felt like crying," a student remarked) in addition to pieces by Chopin and other composers.

The audience responded to Mr. Newson's questions with good humor, and he answered theirs candidly. He started taking piano lessons very late, he said, at nine years of age, when he really preferred to be playing baseball and other sports. He didn't like to practice very much. Somewhere along the way, though, Mr. Newson said he realized that he wasn't going to become a professional athlete. He discovered then that he did have a talent for the piano, and from that point on his serious study of music began.

Mr. Newson prefers informal programs to recitals ("I can't see the faces or anything else beyond the footlights"), but he gives both kinds of programs all over the country. His technical and musical mastery of the keyboard was obvious to everyone. His rapport with the audience was great.

Mr. Newson's appearance in this area was sponsored by the Hale Church Neighborhood Arts Program in Dayton. A phone call from concert coordinator, Virginia Burroughs, put plans for his Yellow Springs visit in motion. We hope it is not the last appearance here. During a potluck supper in his honor, Mr. Newson talked with students and adults, obviously enjoying himself. It was suggested that next year, perhaps, he could return to play a concerto with the Yellow Springs High School Orchestra. My guess is that we have not heard the last of Roosevelt Newson.

## INFORMAL RECITALS

We also have a series of recitals and concerts which occur at school during our regular band and orchestra period. These free performances are given by visiting and local musicians. Other interested students, teachers and townspeople who are available to come are welcome. These are not formal concerts advertised to the general public, but informal programs, sometimes with comments about the music and dialogue with the audience. The recital is in a relaxed setting and given to a knowledgeable audience. Sometimes the artist uses it as a dry-run prior to a public concert. In recent years, we've had visits from a brass quintet, string quartet, woodwind quintet and solo instrumentalists.

## UNIVERSITY PERFORMERS

Area universities use these programs as a highly successful form of recruitment. This includes both recruitment of prospective university students and high school students who may wish to study privately with one of the performers. It's a fact that one of the best ways to entice students to attend their music school is to have students work with their teachers prior to attending college. These programs are often provided free of charge through the extension service of the university. We will occasionally provide lunch and pay mileage, but we seldom pay the group a performance fee. We simply do not have the funds, no matter how valuable we feel the group may be.

Some groups, such as concert bands or symphony orchestras, prefer to play in the auditorium or gymnasium for the entire student body. This kind of performance requires more planning on your part. Most music schools have jazz bands, swing choirs and instrumental ensembles on tour in the spring. If they know you are interested far enough in advance, they may be able to include your school on their itinerary.

## HOSTING TOURING ENSEMBLES

Another possibility for a free concert is to offer to feed and house a touring ensemble. It's an excellent way to establish closer contact with an area music school, and it could easily lead to an exchange concert. Perhaps the following year your group could visit their campus and play for their music education students. We have done this kind of traveling for years and have always found it enjoyable.

The larger the performing group, the more vital the advance planning becomes. A school assembly involves your music supervisor, principal and other teachers. Plan ahead and take advantage of this inexpensive means of broadening your musical offerings. It is certainly worth the time and effort.

These are just a few of the ways we offer live performances to our students. Plan head, check your area's concert schedules, make some phone calls, write some letters, and watch what happens. You should be able to develop an excellent concert series on a shoestring budget.

## Chapter XVI:
# UTOPIA? NOT QUITE!

### "UTOPIA?"

**March 15, 1982**
  *I feel sick.*
  *I went to school early this morning to finish some paper work. Something near my desk smelled. A glass flower vase was full of mud, I thought, but saw that actually it had been filled with dung.*
  *My desk sits out in the hallway of the music department because we're crowded and because I like having it there. In twelve years I've never had any vandalism.*
  *I wondered who was so angry — and why.*

**March 16, 1982**
  *A colleague just called me on the phone. She found a pile of dung on my desk and urine on the floor.*
  *I thought, "Why would anyone be that angry? What will happen next? How can we find the person and help whoever it is."*
  *I went over to see the damage and check on my personal belongings. The person had taken human feces and smeared it over the Beethoven symphony on my desk and on photographs of my teachers and former students. Stunned, I took everything off the walls that remained untouched.*

**March 18, 1982**
  *I just hung everything back up on the wall. I can't live in a shell because someone is sick. Maybe they will leave some sign so we can confront them and help them. I hope so, because someone is walking around ready to explode.*

**June 7, 1982**
  *No recurrence of vandalism. The student remains undetected.*

## UTOPIA? NOT QUITE!

The teaching position you accept after leaving college isn't going to be perfect. Utopias simply don't exist in the real world. Each job position has its pros and cons, and if you decide to change jobs, you may get rid of some problems but you'll surely find others.

### BUILDING A PROGRAM

One of the biggest shocks awaiting new music teachers comes on the very first day of class. *Where are the students?* When you were interviewed last spring, you may have heard a fantastic 70-piece band or 80-voice chorus. Guess what? Over the summer there were some decisions made which you had no control over. Some families moved away, some students had scheduling problems, and of course, the seniors graduated. Things can be rough for any teacher at the first rehearsal in the fall. For the new teachers, it can be devastating.

Look in the music department files to get last year's band and orchestra personnel lists and phone numbers. Cross off the seniors, along with those who have moved. Then start calling the remaining students — *immediately.* If you wait even a few days, they will be settled into their class routine and won't want to reschedule their classes to add music. They will have also started the pairing-off ritual between boys and girls. This is another reason to hurry because potential boyfriends or girlfriends may dictate what classes a student wants to be in. You should be able to pick up a few former members with this personal approach. Then forget the rest and start building your band and your reputation.

### ACCEPT WHAT YOU CAN'T CHANGE

If you visited our music department, you might wonder why we all seem to enjoy teaching there! For one thing, we have completely outgrown our teaching complex. When the building was constructed, the school had an excellent 45-piece concert band. Now, more than 20 years later, we have band, orchestra, show chorus, private teaching studios and an electronic music lab, all in the same facility. We are literally bursting our seams.

Almost every day someone is rehearsing in the hallway or, in good weather, outside. All large group rehearsals are held in the music room, which is too small, poorly ventilated and extremely dead. To make matters worse, our large concerts are all held in the gymnasium. The gym is extremely live, which makes for frustrating problems of balance and sonority. It also has a slight odor of sweat socks which permeates the audience and the performers. Our flower bouquets never completely conceal the fact that we are, indeed, playing in a gym.

We have some minor problems with theft and vandalism because we don't own individual lockers for the students' instruments. They are locked in a large storage room, which is next to the music room. There are students who play pranks, such as switching mouthpieces or hiding someone's music. We will occasionally have a destructive student who will cut the hair from a bow or damage a microphone. Security is a worry for our teaching staff, with incidents of vandalism definitely increasing. Yet, we don't have much deliberate abuse of property compared to that in other schools. I remember giving our new principal the distressing news of some vandalism in the girls' bathroom. When I described it, he was puzzled as to why I was so upset. It would have scarcely been noticed in his former school.

In other words, the physical plant in our music department is far from perfect. It would be nice to have more room, more air, some storage lockers and teaching studios. However, we are all aware that very little can be done to improve the situation. We've simply had to accept the limitations of our facility. The alternative is to be continually frustrated and dissatisfied, diverting our energies from our main purpose of teaching children.

## STRETCHING THE BUDGET

The next problem involves the budget and general funding for the music program. Although music is very strong in our school and the administration supports the programs, there simply isn't enough money to go around. We do not have an adequate budget allowance for instrument purchase, replacement or repair. On occasion, we have been able to combine some foundation gifts with school funds to purchase a handful of instruments, but this has been the exception rather than the rule. All other large and unusual instruments are purchased by the Yellow Springs Youth Orchestra Association. Without its support, the music program could not exist in its present form. Our school system is too small and too strapped financially to carry the program alone.

Our entire instrumental program is largely based on private ownership, with a few instruments available on a scholarship loan basis. I wish we had more and better instruments, but the costs are prohibitive. Our cellos and basses are beginning to deteriorate as repair and replacement costs skyrocket. We do have a serious problem with instrument inventory, both purchase and replacement.

On the other hand, our instrumental music library is quite good. Again, the schools and booster clubs share the expense of music purchase. We spend money carefully in this area because we have to maintain five large ensembles and numerous smaller classes and chamber ensembles. Music prices are very high and will probably continue to rise. Sheet music is high on our priority list. If our budget was reduced in this area, we would fight to reinstate it.

**SCHEDULING**

The problems I've mentioned so far all involve money. They would seem to be major concerns for most people. **My biggest worry is always the same, and it doesn't involve money at all. It's called *scheduling*. This problem will keep me awake nights. It's at the heart of any music program because it determines what day, what time, which children, and even whether you can teach at all.** I once spent the first three weeks of school sitting in the teacher's lounge of a junior high school because the children simply were not available.

Scheduling involves other people who may or may not be interested in having music or any arts program in their school. It involves flexibility, vision, creative thinking, cooperation and a positive approach. This can be an extremely difficult problem, especially in a small school system. Practically speaking, music can be scheduled out with the stroke of a pen and in some instances, this has happened. This may be prompted by expediency and a lack of concern, rather than by malicious intent. Music may be the easiest class to move about, and it may end up in the worse possible time slot. This is a serious problem in high school, where many students have to hold jobs in the afternoon. If band or orchestra is scheduled for the last period and a student has one or two study halls before that, chances are very good that he will drop music. Keep scheduling high on your priority list. Work with the counselor and principal to find a satisfactory solution to this problem.

The school counselor is also the person who will be guiding students in their selection of classes. You must have close ties with the counselor's office. Be sure to give him or her a list of prospective music students prior to registration. There will be some class conflicts, and it will save a lot of time and trouble if the music students are clearly identified. You will also want to check the files of incoming students, especially transfer students from other schools. Most counselors are helpful and want what is best for the student, even if it takes some extra effort to make the schedule work. Yet, you will find an occasional person who will say, "But Frank, what do you want to take music for? You *need* Typing II much more!"

Why am I telling you all these problems about our school when I obviously love my job and my location? I'm telling you because I don't want you to think that everything is perfect. Your roof may leak. Ours does, frequently.

We each have our own personal reasons for choosing where we teach and spend our lives. I enjoy our students and staff above everything. It's a nice place to live and work. People care about each other. The high school is just a five-minute bicycle ride from my home. I can plant flower seeds near my office and no one minds. The large glass windows throughout the school make me feel close to nature all year round. I like the freedom to teach in my own style, never having to look over my shoulder.

**When you consider that new job, look beyond the facility and the salary. Is this a community where you want to live? Do you want to have a family grow up here? Do people like each other? If the answer is "Yes," then grab it!**

# Epilogue

## *TRAVEL*

*We sat on the edge of the bed, weeping and holding each other. "He's gonna die, isn't he? He's gonna die."*

*"No, he's not. You'll see . . . he'll be O.K." I didn't know that at all, but I said it anyway. I wanted to believe it. His friend had passed out in the bathroom and struck his head on the tub. He lay on the floor, cramped and distorted.*

*Two paramedics arrived. They tried to move him but couldn't. He was a football player and a weight lifter and he was too heavy for them. "Can you walk?" one of them asked. He didn't answer but struggled slowly to his feet. He stared blankly into space, then step by step cautiously walked down the motel stairs.*

*The rest of the group had gone ahead, sightseeing with the chaperons. His friend and I went with him in the ambulance. We were so scared. I thought, "He's not a user, I know that. What's wrong with him? What's happened?"*

*We called his mother back home and she explained. "He's an epileptic and he must have forgotten to take his medicine. He has to take it every night . . . Don't cry. It's not your fault. He's a young man, not a baby."*

*Hours later he opened his eyes, smiled and said, "Hey, what's with the long faces?" His friend and I looked at each other and grinned. It had been a very long day.*

# MEET MARIA

*"What do you want for lunch today?" she asked.*
*"Oh, Maria, I'm kind of rushed. How about a salad and an apple and oh, a chocolate milk."*
*"O.K. See you later."*
*This might be a typical exchange between a student and a teacher anywhere . . . except that the student is in a wheelchair. The fact that I don't even question how she is going to navigate my lunch through two heavy glass doors describes my growth over the past two years.*

*Maria came into my life during our Summer String Program. The only difference with her application and dozens of others was that it had a note attached. It said that she would be having an operation during June and would have to start violin lessons late. It also explained that she was homebound and would need to be tutored.*

*I was a little nervous the first time I went to see Maria. I had never taught a child in a wheelchair before, and I wasn't sure what to expect. Her mother greeted me at the door with a big smile and a beautiful Italian accent. Maria was waiting for me in the living room. It became apparent immediately that she was intelligent, sensitive, and had a great sense of humor. We quickly discovered we shared the common experience of raising rabbits. Her mother served tea and cookies while we talked.*

*Then the lesson began. We both felt a little awkward but we soon figured out how to avoid the arm of the wheelchair. When I said, "Tap your foot," we both laughed and counted out loud instead. That was the beginning. Since that day, Maria has changed. We have all changed.*

*She takes violin lessons at school now with a high school student teacher, joining in with the intermediate orchestra once a week. She plays in concerts and recitals; she comes to other high school programs and activities. She gets "dolled up" and flirts shamelessly with the boys. She has become independent.*

*Maria is coming down the hall, bringing my lunch — plus a double-decker chocolate ice cream cone!*

## THE VIOLINIST

*The concert was almost ready to begin when I noticed her standing at the bottom of the stairs. She looked beautiful in her long blue gown, new for this special occasion. The rest of the orchestra was already on stage, tuning and getting settled.*

*"Mary Anne, are you ready?" I asked. She glanced at me, looked down, and said nothing. Her face was firey red and she was completely frozen in time and space. "Of course," I thought. "This is her first concert." I took her arm in mine and together we walked up the steps. Then, like a baby bird, she flew away on her own.*

## *ANGER*

This happened yesterday.
High school orchestra had just finished. It was a good rehearsal, full of energy and emotional highs and lows. I was relaxing, discussing things with my student teacher. I glanced up and saw a young girl walking through the doorway. Her arms were full of books and instruments. She was sobbing. She ran to me and I held her while she wept. People stood quietly, watching and listening. It was beautiful and strange, this quiet in the middle of the rush between classes.
She told me what had happened. Two boys had backed her into a corner and had looked down her blouse. She didn't know why. She hadn't done anything to make them mad at her. She was angry and frightened.
Soon, she quieted down and her heart stopped pounding. She said something remarkable. "It was a bad thing . . . a dumb thing . . . but I could have handled it. But they LIED about it. They said I had pulled up my blouse. They told that story to their friends. They LIED about me." She's tough and she'll be O.K. She understands their problem.
It happened twelve hours ago and I am still angry . . . I will always be angry.

## *TRAVEL BROADENS ONE'S HORIZONS*

"This is the perfect dormitory housing," I thought. Our orchestra had spent a busy day visiting a university music school and we were all exhausted. I was getting ready to take bed check, finding it handy to have the students all on one floor. It was a V-shaped corridor with boys on one side and girls on the other. I was remembering with horror a motel where the roofs between adjacent buildings were the perfect height for Tarzan feats of daring.

"Roll call, everybody — listen, please:
Polly, Lynn, Jimmy, Robbie, Mollye, . . . SWISH, SWISH, SWISH!"

Three total strangers raced past my clip board like whirling dervishes. I saw three brightly colored mufflers, three handsome bodies, and three absolutely bare bottoms! One poor fellow tripped and fell. His university buddies abandoned him, of course, and he made a hasty retreat.

I continued with roll call . . . "Karin, Simone, Felix, Wendy . . . Good night, everyone. See you in the morning."

I went into my room and shut the door. Then the laughter burst out. It seems that we had arrived for our brief visit right in the heyday of campus streaking. As they always say, "Travel broadens your horizons!"

## SKETCH IN BLACK AND WHITE

It was Martin Luther King day and we had just played for the school assembly. The crowd was hushed, waiting for the guest speaker to begin. Suddenly, I heard an ugly voice. It wasn't a shout but it was loud enough for most people to hear. "We don't need your white face around here!"

After the program was over, my principal put his arm around my shoulder. "Never mind," he said. "My little girl answered the phone this morning to, "Hey, nigger — who in the hell was Martin Luther King?"

## *THE RECITAL*

It had been a long week. It had been a long Spring. It had been a long year! The final recital was here and I wished it were over.

I had taught all day, given four lessons after school, and had to be back early for the program. That left one hour to grab a bite, hug the kids, kiss my husband, feed the dog, take a shower and dress. Sometimes I wonder why I stay in this rat race.

It was a nice program. Everyone played well and it was almost over. "Thank heavens," I thought. "I can go home to my bed, stretch out, and read for awhile."

Then it happened. Three seniors I'd known since they were children played a Brahms horn trio. It was just one movement, it was just a recital, and it was incredibly beautiful. When they had finished and the audience had left, I asked if they would play it again, just for me.

They played and suddenly, there was my answer. That's why we all stay in this "rat race." We are the lucky ones.

## *THE ANSWER*

One of my favorite students dropped orchestra one day, suddenly and without an explanation. I was puzzled and secretly felt hurt. So I asked the question. "Why? Why did you quit? I want to know because it will make me a better teacher." Nothing could have prepared me for the quick reply. "It was a waste of my time, and I didn't learn a thing." Silently, I watched the bike and the backpack disappear down the road.

Sometimes when I think I have all the answers, I remember that day. I see the eyes and I hear the words — the tone of voice, the inflection — and I feel the hurt all over.

It's good to remember and to feel and to learn. It makes me a better teacher.

# CONCLUSION

A young man wearing a floppy cowboy hat adorned with a crumpled feather wandered into the music room four days before he was to graduate from high school. He looked at me and said, "I've been a fool to miss this opportunity . . . will you teach me the cello?" I was busy, tired and annoyed, but I grabbed an old cello and said, "Sit on the edge of your chair, lean slightly forward, put your left foot . . . " Why did I do it? Because he wanted to learn something about the cello, that's why.

As you've finished reading this odd assortment of bits and pieces of human experience, you might wonder, Why did I write this book? What were my intentions? Where are the answers? Where are the chapter questions and the study sheets?

I'm sorry to disappoint you, but there are no answers, no seating charts, no lesson plans, no "sure-fire" recruiting techniques. Surely you can find those things in other books among the excellent sources on the market. No, that's not why I wrote this book, suffering through the pain of writing, rewriting, editing and rejecting.

**I wrote it to remember the human qualities which make teaching worthwhile and important. I wrote it because we need to love our students. I wrote it to help young teachers understand what teaching is about.**

As I said before, it's a great way to spend a lifetime.

# CONCLUSION

# INDEX

Attitudes, 1, 2, 31-41
  and body language, 34-36
  importance of, 33
  interpretation of, 34-36
  negative, 32-39, 58, 63
  of parents, 38-39
  positive, 2, 32-34, 38-39
  professional, 3, 11-12
  and selection of music, 38
  of students, 33-34, 37-39, 40
  of teachers, 32-33, 36, 37, 57, 73
  towards music program, 11, 63, 73
Administrators, 10-15
  and budgets, 85
  communicating with, 11-12
  credibility with, 13
  motivation of, 48
  presenting ideas to, 13-14, 48
  requests in writing to, 26, 48
Adjudicators, 53, 57-58. *See also* Contests
Accompanists, 55. *See also* Contests
Auditions, 59, 62
  for seating, 63
Artist series, 91-94
  finding performers for, 91

Behavior problems, 1, 15, 17, 34, 40
  and classroom standards, 17
  and responsibility, 28
  *See also* Discipline
Body language, 34-36

Boosters' clubs, 81, 97. *See also* Funding
Budgets, 11, 97. *See also* Funding

Challenge system. *See* Auditions
Clinics, 7
Classroom control, 16. *See also* Discipline
Communication, 4
  and administrators, 11
  and stage presence, 23
Community service, 58, 74-75
Community support, 87
Competitions, young artists', 6, 58, 62
  *See also* Contests
Compositions, student, 65, 66
Colleagues, 7
  and conflict, 2
  and organizations, 6
Concert artists, 90-92. *See also* Artist series
Conferences, parent/teacher, 38-39, 48-49
Confidence, 23. *See also* Stage presence
Conflict, 1-4
  and flexibility, 28
  and scheduling, 28
  *See also* Discipline; Confrontation
Confrontation, 40-41
Cooperation, 2. *See also* Flexibility

# INDEX

Counselor, teacher as, 24-26
Conventions, 7, 12
Creativity, 13, 14

Discipline, 15-18
   and anger, 1, 2, 15, 17, 105
   and classroom flexibility, 17
   and conflict, 1
   establishing rules of, 16-17
   and fear, 18
   parent notification of problem in, 3
   and sarcasm, 18
   setting parameters of, 16
   styles in teaching, 16
   and teaching techniques, 17, 29
Drop-outs, 39, 51-52, 63, 109

Ensembles, student, 30, 31, 37, 55, 60, 75
   and travel, 82, 94
      *See also* Contests

Fellowships. *See* Funding
Festivals. *See* Contests
Flexibility, 2, 27-30, 66
   and classroom pacing, 30-31
   and conflicts, 28
   and teaching methods, 27, 29, 30, 42
Foundations, 84
Friendships, 25-26
   with students, 24, 25
   with former students, 26
Funding, 80-85, 97
   by boosters' clubs, 81-82
   by foundations, 4, 84
Fund raising. *See* Funding

Gifted students. *See* Students, gifted
Grants, 84-85
   Guide to applying for, 84

Judge's comments, 53, 57-58
   *See also* Contests

Listening, 16
   and flexibility, 28-29
   and students' problems, 25, 35-36

Master class, 91, 92
Methods, teaching. *See* Teaching techniques

Misunderstandings, between colleagues, 3
Motivation, 38, 42-52, 54
   of administrators, 48
   and contests, 54, 58
   failure of, 51-52
   and fear, 48
   of key students, 48
   parents approach to, 44
   and performances, 48
   and private lessons, 44-45
   and seating, 48
   techniques of, 45-47

Negative attitudes. *See* Attitudes
Nervousness, and performance, 22, 27, 59, 104

Orchestras, youth, 61-63
Organization
   of tasks, 3-4, 17, 61
   of time, 3-4, 17
Organizations
   booster, 81-83
   local, 8
   professional, 5, 6, 54

Pacing
   and teaching methods, 17, 29-30
   and homework assignments, 29
Parents
   attitudes towards music program, 38, 39
   and motivation, 44, 45
Parent/teacher conferences, 38, 48
Performances
   and nervousness, 22, 27, 59, 104
   professional, 6, 8, 20, 90, 91, 94
   student, 19, 23, 37, 53, 58, 60, 72, 75, 77, 108
Planning, 3, 17. *See also* Organization; Discipline
Positions, teaching, 96-99
Positive attitudes. *See* Attitudes
Practicing, 44-45
Press releases, 86-87, 93. *See also* Public relations
Private instruction
   for students, 44-45, 65, 76
   for teachers, 8, 65, 76

# INDEX

Problems
  anger, 2, 15
  in new positions, 96-98
  of students, 25, 102
  vandalism, 95, 96
    *See also* Discipline
Public relations, 13, 38, 48, 86-89

Recitals, informal, 67-68, 84, 93, 94, 108
Recruiting, 72-79, 96
  and community service, 74, 75
  formal method of, 75, 76
  importance of, 73, 96
  and performances, 77, 94
Rehearsals, 31, 32
  with accompanists, 56
  and sight-reading, 55
  techniques of conducting, 7, 37, 38
Rules, 16
  and contests, 53, 54
  and exceptions, 16
  and flexibility, 28, 29

Scheduling, 11, 98-99
Seating, 47, 63
Sight-reading, 17, 54-55
Stage presence, 19-24, 57, 58
  and clothing, 21
  and confidence, 20, 29
  and personal magnetism, 22
  and personal style, 21
  and relaxed manner, 20
  teaching basic elements of, 23

Students, gifted, 58-71
  and composing, 65
  identifying, 60
  performances of, 58, 60-61
Students as teachers, 66-71
Student teachers, 16
Supplementary teaching materials, 30

Teachers
  attitudes of, 32, 33
  as friends and counselors, 24-26
  students as, 66-71
Teacher's pets, 25-26
Teaching positions, problems of, 96-99
Teaching techniques, 7, 29-30
  and flexibility, 29
  and gifted students, 60-71
  and pacing, 30
  and sight-reading, 55
  and small ensembles, 29-30
  of student teachers, 68-71
    *See also* Flexibility
Touring Ensembles. *See* Ensembles

Workshops, 7, 12

Young artists' competitions, 58, 62
Youth orchestras, 62-63